THE BATHERS'
PAVILION
CAFÉ
COOKBOOK

THE BATHERS' PAVILION

CAFÉ COOKBOOK

Serge Dansereau   Photographs by Petrina Tinslay

ABC
Books

CONTENTS

To my great staff at Bathers'
who give me so much support

and to

Yvette, Celéste and Sasha
who bring me so much joy at home

———————————————————————————

I moved to Balmoral in 1996 because my dream was to live on the beach. I had been married to Yvette for four years but we still lived apart: she was busy in Melbourne running her business and I never seemed to have a weekend or night off. This move to Balmoral was going to give us the chance to finally live together and build a home.

I loved the warm water and the white sand

 of Sydney's beaches, and Balmoral was one of the most picturesque. Every night, after I finished work, Yvette and I would go for a late walk on the promenade that fronted our beachfront apartment. It was relaxing, walking to the sound of the gentle waves or the screech of the bats under the huge fig trees, while the seagulls tried to catch a nap on the highwire of the shark net.

The highlight of our walk was seeing the happy customers in the rustic setting of The Bathers' Pavilion. We smelt the wood burning in the fireplace and saw the patrons appreciating one of the great restaurants of Sydney. More than once it crossed my mind that it would be fantastic to work at such a place. The unique architecture made me curious about its history and about the time when the building was used for its original purpose.

Balmoral's development was slow compared to the rest of Sydney, due to its lack of viable transport. In the late 1800s, Balmoral was a well-known artists' camp, sharing space with Aboriginal and Chinese bush camps and a few private lots, but eventually the tram and buses reached the suburb and transformed the place.

Balmoral's natural assets — the surfless beaches of Hunters Bay, the soft sand dunes and the enchanted setting facing Sydney Heads — attracted crowds of picnickers and bathers, especially in the summer months. More public space was needed for the

gentlemen and ladies of the era to indulge in their recreation, and so Balmoral Park was created in 1886; this was followed by the repossession of private land by Mosman Municipal Council along the bay. The Council erected bathing facilities due to the ever-growing influx of visitors to the beach and the resort atmosphere of Balmoral.

By 1924, trams, motorbuses and ferry services from Circular Quay fully serviced the beach and the suburb. The Balmoral tramline was opened in May 1922, making its way from Spit Junction to Middle Head Road and down to Balmoral Beach, ending at Lawry Parade (which was later renamed The Esplanade). The tram terminus was near the present bus stop at the south end of Rocky Point (the island). Even before The Bathers' Pavilion opened, it was calculated that the beach crowd could reach over thirty thousand people in summer, many tens of thousands more than there are these days. There was a boat rental business, Treimuth's dressing sheds, the Beach Club, the ferry wharf, Shearers Baths, the boat shed, a dance hall called Happyland and Cavills Baths.

The bathing phenomenon took hold of Sydney, putting continued pressure on its accessible beaches. On seeing the proliferation of swimming clubs, sheds and bathing activities, Mosman Municipal Council had to react to this demand and did so by commissioning a state-of-the-art bathing pavilion. The main pressure for this development was the moral obligation to provide adequate facilities. Social mores of the day were quite strict and conservative and the building of a pavilion made the activity of mixed-sex bathing seem more acceptable.

In 1924 Lawry Parade was completed, and in the process many majestic trees were cut down. An English-style promenade was quickly built, as well as a band rotunda, with the help of funds earmarked to alleviate the unemployment created by the Great Depression. The laying of concrete was another controversial decision as it replaced the sand dunes of the beach and necessitated the cutting down of many more trees. It was the start of a groundswell of opposition to the perception of a council that was intent on concreting the beaches over; the public campaign of opposition to this development meant that many councillors did not survive their next election.

At the same time, The Bathers' Pavilion was commissioned to be built by Mosman Municipal Council. The Council's architect and building surveyor, Alfred Hale, designed the building, and Alderman Harry Carter laid the foundation stone on 21 August 1928. The design was certainly seductive in its external shell, with its distinct and intriguing Moorish feel and intricate features, such as the many delicate fretwork windows, which had to provide privacy and ventilation. Alfred Hale's design made what was essentially a large changing shed a stunning and imposing visual adornment to the beach. The Pavilion was officially opened on 20 February 1929.

The Bathers' Pavilion was set over two storeys, catering for men, women and boys. It had living quarters for the caretaker, and an ambulance and attendant's room. The north side of the building was used for the women and the south side for the men. From day one the building was leased to a private operator. Woollen bathing costumes, caps, towels and trunks were made available for a fee, as well as 1506 lockers and 239 changeroom cubicles where one could disrobe in privacy. The building was advertised as possessing the latest sanitary conveniences. The boys' area was later subleased and used for the sale of refreshments, causing a big controversy at the time.

More controversial was the building of the shark barrier. There were plenty of blue pointers and bronze whalers cruising the deep channel up to The Spit and a shark attack would have had a devastating effect on the well-established business of the beach. In 1926 the Council considered an application to build a Blackpool-style pier extending right across Edwards Beach from Rocky Point to the Wyargine rocks on the north side of the beach, where a four-storey edifice was to be built, dwarfing The Bathers' Pavilion. It was rejected mostly over the issue of giving a private body power over access to the beach. The next proposal was to build a wooden shark-proof barrier along the full length of Edwards Beach. This proposal was also rejected because it included fencing off the beach and charging an entrance fee.

It was not until 1935, following a spate of dramatic and fatal shark attacks on Sydney beaches, that the present shark net was built. It was one-quarter of the originally proposed size. Many swimmers opted to swim outside it, but the Council could no longer ignore the menace of shark attack. The last fatal attack was in January 1955 in clear view of The Bathers' Pavilion. A thirteen-year-old boy entered the water with some meat to bait his lobster pot, despite the warning from another swimmer that a large shark had been seen prowling the area over the last few days. John Willis was fatally attacked. With the netting of those beaches that were inside Sydney Heads, shark attacks and sightings eventually diminished and became a rarity.

The use of The Bathers' Pavilion remained pretty much as originally intended until the late 1960s, when there was 'a sharp decline in the use made by the public' of the building's changing facilities. Mr Kenaef won the tender and established the well-known Mischa's Restaurant, a place that is still fondly remembered by many. 'Mischa', as he was called, traded from 1979–1986 without realising his dream of a second-floor restaurant, but he made brunch an institution at Balmoral.

Not long after Yvette and I had moved into our Balmoral apartment, I could not help but notice the controversy that raged over the renovation of the Pavilion. The lease of The Bathers' Pavilion had been purchased by Andrew Joseph and his wife Victoria Alexander. Their intention was to create a small hotel, make use of the whole dilapidated building and provide the funds for the Council to renew the fabric of the building. The building was in dire need of renovation and the proposal seemed to be a perfect use of an historic building, so I found it hard to understand the opposition. Sure, it probably made sense to reserve part of the building for the community's use, but what type of use: teaching crafts, group meetings, lectures, or some other limited use? The Council had plenty of unused rooms and spaces in their community centre and could not justify using this prime location to do what could easily be done at other buildings.

Fear was another major factor that contributed to the public's objection to the project. Was it going to be a large bar with drunken people spilling out late at night? Was it going to be a hotel with all the seedy activities that could go on there, or was it going to be an elitist place for the wealthy few? Add to that the fear that it would attract more people to Balmoral Beach, with its limited parking facilities, and the mix was a potent one, full of misinformation and uninformed judgment. The debate became very public, protracted, costly and divisive, which is quite common when a much-loved, historical and public building is at stake.

The process of resolution went through an interminable succession of Council meetings, legal challenges and negotiations over many years. The fact that it was going to be a commercial development (thereby allowing the Council to renovate the derelict building) was probably never in question. The real issues were just what type of business was going to occupy the space and was any of the space to be allocated for public use. All of these issues were resolved in the late 1990s when the last legal challenge was finally exhausted, allowing the work to proceed.

Victoria's dream was to design and develop a small hotel. Her vision would preserve the fabric of the building with its strong but lost link to the area and make use of the entire floor space for activities that seemed compatible with the site. It would also provide a regular income for the Council and anchor the building in renewed and replanted parkland. Her tenacity became legendary, even though she eventually had to give away the hotel portion of her dream and replace it with a larger restaurant.

I received Victoria's call to ask me to be part of the redevelopment of Bathers' while I was travelling in France. I knew the building well and had an admiration for her commitment to preserving it. I also admired her sense of style and the way she had created such a beautiful and cosy place. It was a restaurant with a great view, good food and the many touches that defined her design. It had a distinct style that people loved: the view, the food, the wine, and the casual but informed service; it all made for a restaurant that was quintessential Sydney.

On my return from my trip I agreed to form an equal partnership with Victoria to design, build and operate the new Pavilion and become the new lessees of this iconic building. Her role was to style the place and my role was to cook and run the operation. It was a dream come true, even though we eventually parted ways. I was living a few minutes walk from the site on the same street and I was ready to take on a new challenge after working at The Regent, Sydney for so many years. I finally had the chance to design my own kitchens, develop menus, select table settings, hire

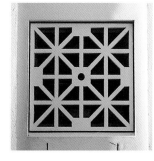

my own staff and create great food directly in front of one of Sydney's most beautiful beaches. It was going to be a magnificently rewarding project.

I knew the people who came to Balmoral Beach: it was full of local walkers, out-of-suburb strollers and the hard-core swimmers and health fanatics. The Café would have to be child-friendly as it was the families and the people who worked from home who came to the beach during the day. The menu in the Café was going to be Mediterranean in style, with wood-fired pizza, vegetables, salad, risotto and fresh seafood prepared simply. I was not prepared to mix styles to become an Australian bistro that serves everything; I wanted to concentrate on cooking in a clear style, with dishes that highlighted the quality of our local produce.

Before the renovation could start to provide a functional space for a restaurant, a lot of the fabric had to be preserved, renovated and readapted. Robert A. Moore was the heritage consultant who understood the history of the building, and also understood the need to have a person of great sensitivity to produce an integral design that would satisfy many competing objectives. The design had to be functional but, more importantly, it had to respect the integrity and the history of the building.

Alex Popov was appointed as architect in charge of producing the design. He had a reputation for his stylish and intelligent home design, incorporating and blending in a zen-like fashion the concepts of light, space and shelter. Alex created an intelligent design of great simplicity and I found my time working with him very inspiring. Alex's design legacy has fulfilled so thoughtfully our need for heritage respect, practicality and a sense of space.

Once the spatial arrangements were firmed, then the hard work of defining and developing the architectural interiors started. Grant McConnell and John Rayner from McConnell Rayner (architects) were the last link in the production of our dream restaurant. In June 1999, after a huge amount of planning, design, demolition and reconstruction with all the intricate work involved, The Bathers' Pavilion finally reopened, providing pleasure to the many who were to patronise this great building and unique restaurant.

People love driving over the top of Balmoral Hill as the curve of Hunters Bay reveals itself with the glittering sea, national parks and

Sydney heads in the distance. By the time you reach the bottom of the hill the historic Bathers' Pavilion and its promenade give the feel of a different era. Set in the picturesque harbour shores and framed by its parkland and the stunning Port Jackson and Moreton Bay fig trees, it is a unique vista.

Once you enter The Bathers' Pavilion, the first thing you notice is the beach view, which offers an overwhelming background to the clean line of the restaurant and café. The proximity of the beach is a constant reminder of the link between a beach pavilion and the reinvented Bathers'. While the historic building has now clearly outlived its original purpose, a new life has been breathed into its fabric. It is such a unique experience to sit in the café or restaurant and absorb the view and the activities of the beach and the bay, with its ever-present beach-goers and boats sailing in the distance. And more than once we have been graced with the presence of whales and dolphins in full view of Bathers'.

The Café has been such a success because the public loves the food on offer and the casual but efficient service we provide. Yes, the views are gorgeous, but bad food would prevent them from returning. My role is to bring joy to all my customers, to make Sydneysiders proud of what we have to offer and to create a workplace that reflects the best Australia can provide in terms of food, wine and service.

The recipes in this book are all from the Bathers' Café and they are the type of food that I enjoy cooking and my patrons love to eat. They are recipes that are approachable and designed to be enjoyed and cooked in your kitchen. I hope it will help you take home a little of The Bathers' Pavilion.

Bon appétit
Serge Dansereau

Morning at Bathers'

is a refreshing swim or gentle walk on the sandy beach,

a freshly baked basket of exquisite pastries, the smell

of fresh coffee, indulging in fluffy pancakes or a Belgian

hot chocolate; it is a chance to slowly ease into the day

and absorb the smells, sights and sounds of the sea ...

toasted panettone with fresh berries and mascarpone

Serves 4

200 g (7 oz) fresh mascarpone
  cheese
50 ml (1½ fl oz) fresh cream
200 g (7 oz) icing sugar
4 handfuls of mixed summer berries,
  eg. strawberries, blueberries,
  raspberries, blackberries

Panettone

40 g (1½ oz) mixed peel
zest of 1 orange
1 dash Marsala
16 g (½ oz) fresh yeast or
  8 g (¼ oz) dry yeast
100 ml (3½ fl oz) milk at body
  temperature (36° C)
1 tsp sugar
500 g (1 lb) bakers flour
2 tbs sugar
1 pinch salt
1 egg
2 drops vanilla essence
40 g (1½ oz) soft butter
140 g (4½ oz) sultanas

To make panettone, place mixed peel and zest in a bowl and pour over Marsala. Leave to soak for 2 hours.

Combine yeast, milk and 1 tsp sugar and leave somewhere warm until foam appears (approximately 15 minutes).

Place flour, remaining sugar, salt, egg and vanilla essence in a bowl and mix in the yeast starter. Mix into a moist, but not too sticky dough and knead for 5–10 minutes until smooth and elastic, or use a bread machine to mix.

Add the butter and finally the sultanas and zest. Mix well.

Cover with cling film and leave in a warm place to double in volume. This should take about 45 minutes –1½ hours, depending on the weather.

Knock back and shape into a greased loaf tin. Bake at 200°C for 35 – 45 minutes or until loaf sounds hollow when tapped on the base. Turn out and cool on a wire rack.

To serve, mix mascarpone with cream and sugar.

Cut 1 cm thick slices of panettone and toast until lighly golden. Place on serving plates.

Scatter berries on and around the panettone, and top with a dollop of mascarpone cream. Dust with icing sugar if you like.

blueberry pancakes

Serve these fancy pancakes when friends drop in for breakfast

Serves 4

6 eggs

250 ml (1 cup) milk

150 g (5 oz) sugar

1 tsp vanilla essence

350 g (11½ oz) plain flour

2 tbsp baking powder

1 tsp yoghurt

1 cup fresh or frozen blueberries, crushed

maple syrup

Separate eggs. Whisk together milk, sugar, vanilla and egg yolks, then add flour and baking powder. Mix until smooth.

Whisk egg whites until stiff peaks form. Fold one-third of egg white mixture and the yoghurt into batter with a wooden spoon until well combined, then gently fold through the rest of the egg whites. Add crushed blueberries.

Heat a crêpe pan or nonstick frying pan over low to medium heat. Brush the pan with a little butter and cook the pancakes one at a time.

For each pancake, ladle ¼ cup of batter into the pan and cook for about 2 minutes, or until bubbles appear on the surface. Turn the pancake over and cook for another minute. Transfer to a plate and keep warm while cooking the rest of the pancakes.

Serve the pancakes in stacks with plenty of maple syrup.

croque monsieur

Serves 4

8 slices of country bread
   or sourdough
100 g (3½ oz) soft butter
1 tbsp seeded mustard
16 slices leg ham off
   the bone
16 slices gruyère cheese
cracked pepper to taste
oven-roasted tomatoes
   (see recipe page 200)

Butter each slice of bread on one side, turn over and spread some mustard on the unbuttered side. Take 4 peices and on each side that has mustard, top with the ham, the cheese and some cracked pepper. Top with the remaining bread slice (mustard side down).

Cover with plastic wrap and refrigerate for 30 minutes to firm up. In a cast iron or nonstick pan, panfry the croque monsieur on a medium heat on both sides until golden.

Serve hot with oven-roasted tomatoes.

cheese on toast

Serves 4

100 ml (3½ fl oz) beer
1 tbsp Worcestershire sauce
250 g (8 oz) grated cheese
1 tbsp English mustard
salt and pepper
4 thick slices of grain bread
2 halves of grilled tomato
chopped chives to garnish

Gently warm the beer and the Worcestershire sauce without boiling. Remove from heat and stir in the cheese until it is thoroughly combined and smooth. Add the mustard and season to taste.

Pour the mixture into a container to set. The mix will keep in the fridge for up to 5 days. Spread onto toast and grill until golden.

Serve with grilled tomatoes and finely chopped chives.

spring vegetable tarts with poached eggs and hollandaise sauce

Serves 4

Spring Vegetable Tarts

4 shortcrust pastry tart bases
   (see recipe page 197)

8 asparagus stalks

8 snowpeas

150 g (5 oz) green peas

16 sugar snap peas

1 small bunch watercress

4 stems broccolini

4 eggs

1 quantity of hollandaise sauce
   (see recipe page 194)

To make vegetable tarts, preheat oven to 180°C. Roll out pastry 2 mm thick and cut 16 cm rounds to line 8 cm greased pie pans. Cook tart bases until golden brown.

Bring a saucepan of salted water to the boil and blanch all vegetables until just cooked but still bright in colour. Remove immediately and strain on paper towel. Sprinkle with salt. Poach the eggs.

To serve, place vegetables into warm pastry cases. Place the poached eggs on top of vegetables. Spoon over hollandaise sauce, then serve.

granola

Serves 6

50 g (1½ oz) brown sugar

75 ml (2½ fl oz) honey

1 tbsp oil

2 drops vanilla essence

250 g (8 oz) oats

35 g (1 oz) desiccated coconut

85 g (3 oz) almonds, chopped

30 g (1 oz) sunflower seeds

30 g (1 oz) pumpkin seeds

Preheat oven to 120°C.

Bring the sugar, honey, oil and vanilla to the boil in a large saucepan. Remove from heat.

Place all other ingredients in a bowl and mix well. Pour the hot sugar mix over the dry ingredients and stir well until dry mix is coated.

Spread over an oven tray and bake for 40 minutes or until golden brown.

Store in an airtight container if not using straightaway.

bircher muesli

Serves 4 to 6

250 g (8 oz) rolled oats

500 ml (2 cups) milk

125 ml (½ cup) cream

100 ml (3½ fl oz) orange juice

1 tbsp lemon juice

90 ml (3 fl oz) honey

2 grated apples

2 diced oranges

80 g (3 oz) sultanas

50 g (1½ oz) slivered roasted almonds

125 g (4 oz) natural yoghurt

Soak the oats in all the liquids. Add the rest of ingredients and leave overnight in the fridge before use. Top this with a brunoise (small dice) of different melons or fresh berries.

strawberry and watermelon jelly with citrus salad

Serves 4

Strawberry and Watermelon Jelly
4 leaves of gelatine
500 ml (2 cups) fresh watermelon
    juice
150 g (5 oz) sugar
dash of lemon juice
4 strawberries

Citrus Salad
1 ruby grapefruit
1 pomelo
1 large orange
2 limes
1 blood orange
1 cup cream (gently whipped) to serve

To make jelly, soak gelatine leaves in $^1/_2$ cup of cold water until soft. Warm a small quantity of watermelon juice with the sugar and stir until sugar is dissolved. Add the softened gelatine leaves to melt. Strain and add to the rest of the watermelon juice with the lemon juice. Allow to cool.

Place 4 strawberry quarters in the base of 4 one-cup ramekins, or use 4 glasses. Pour a small quantity of the warm jelly over the strawberries and set in the fridge. Add the balance of the jelly. Return to fridge and allow to set.

To make citrus salad, peel then slice or segment the citrus fruits.

To serve, break up jelly with a small spoon to achieve a marbled effect in the glass. Add citrus fruits and top with the blood orange. Serve topped with the whipped cream.

fromage blanc with poached pears

Serves 4

Fromage Blanc
1 litre (4 cups) milk
1 tbsp natural yoghurt
2 plain junket tablets
1 tbsp cold water

Poached Pears
400 ml (13 fl oz) water
400 g (13 oz) sugar
1/2 vanilla bean
1 cinnamon quill
4 pears, peeled

To make fromage blanc, warm the milk until it is tepid to warm (no more than 36°C). Whisk the yoghurt into the warmed milk.

Dissolve the junket tablets in cold water, stir into the milk and leave in a warm place overnight (on top of a warm fridge or near a warm oven). The mixture will set to the consistency of soft jelly, forming a curd. (**Note:** if it is too cold the fromage blanc will not set and if it is too hot it will become too firm.)

Place the curd in a square of cheesecloth to drain. Hang on a kitchen tap over a bowl in the sink, or pour into a colander lined with the cheesecloth, over a shallow tray. Allow the curd to drain for several hours.

To make poached pears, in a medium-sized saucepan combine the water, sugar, vanilla bean and cinnamon. Stir to dissolve the sugar and bring to the boil.

Remove the core from the pears by scooping with a teaspoon from the base. Place the pears in the poaching liquid, cover with waxed paper and simmer until cooked. This should take 10–15 minutes, depending on the size and ripeness of the pears.

Cool and drain. Serve poached pear with a little of the poaching liquid and a spoon of the fromage blanc.

deep-fried apple rings with honey and raisin ricotta

Serves 4

150 g (5 oz) dried raisins

100 ml (3$\frac{1}{2}$ fl oz) Sauternes wine
   or water

200 g (7 oz) fresh ricotta cheese

4 granny smith apples

Saffron Batter

2 eggs

2 drops vanilla essence

100 g (3$\frac{1}{2}$ oz) sugar

400 ml (13 fl oz) milk

200 g (7 oz) plain flour

1 tsp baking powder

100 g (3$\frac{1}{2}$ oz) cornflour

pinch of saffron powder

extra flour, for coating apple rings

100 ml (3$\frac{1}{2}$ fl oz) honey

ground cinnamon

Presoak raisins with Sauternes wine or water until the fruit is plump (about 1 hour). Strain off excess liquid. Mix soaked raisins with ricotta cheese. Cover and place in fridge.

Peel and core apples, then cut into 1–2 cm thick slices. Set aside until later.

To make saffron batter, break eggs into a bowl, then add vanilla and sugar. Mix until sugar has dissolved. Add milk, flour, baking powder, cornflour and saffron powder and mix to a thick batter.

Dust apple rings with flour, then toss into batter to coat. Take each apple ring and deep fry in vegetable oil heated to 180°C. Cook until golden brown. Remove from oil and drain on paper towel.

To serve, place apple rings on plate, top with a spoon of ricotta and raisin mixture. Drizzle with honey and sprinkle with cinnamon.

smoked salmon on corn fritters

Serves 4

3 cobs of corn
2 medium potatoes, peeled,
    parboiled, then grated
handful of finely chopped mint,
    parsley and coriander
handful of finely chopped
    spring onion
1 egg, lightly beaten
salt and pepper
1 tbsp oil
1 quantity of creamed corn
    (see recipe page 199)
8 slices of smoked salmon
rocket leaves
extra virgin olive oil
cracked black pepper

Preheat oven to 160°C. Presoak cobs of corn in cold water for 15 minutes, then roast in oven for 20 minutes. Let cobs cool, then remove husks and strip kernels from the cob. Mix the roasted corn kernels, potatoes, herbs, and spring onion with the lightly beaten egg. Season to taste.

Heat oil in a nonstick pan. Place a greased egg ring in pan and fill with the mix. Fry until golden then turn and cook on other side. Set aside in a warm place. Repeat with remaining mixture until all the fritter mixture is cooked.

Divide the heated creamed corn between serving plates and top with corn fritters.

Top the fritters with slices of smoked salmon and a pile of rocket leaves. Drizzle with extra virgin olive oil and top the finished dish with cracked pepper. Serve immediately.

slow-cooked pineapple crêpes with ginger and ricotta

Serves 4

Crêpes
2 eggs
50 g (1½ oz) sugar
1 pinch salt
250 ml (1 cup) milk
75 g (2½ oz) plain flour

Crêpe Filling
1 medium-sized ripe pineapple
150 g (5 oz) chopped
crystallised ginger
200 g (7 oz) sugar
2 vanilla beans, cut in half
lengthways
500 ml (2 cups) water
200 g (7 oz) fresh ricotta

To make crêpes, mix the eggs with the sugar, salt and milk until sugar has dissolved, then add flour, mixing until batter is smooth. The batter should be very liquid.

Heat a lightly-greased nonstick frying pan or crêpe pan, then add a ladle (¼ cup) of the crêpe batter, moving the pan around so that the batter runs all over the bottom of the pan. Cook crêpe until brown. Turn over and brown the other side. Remove and set aside to cool, then repeat to make a total of eight crêpes.

To make filling, peel and core pineapple. Cut into 2.5 cm cubes. Place into a medium-sized pot with ginger, sugar, vanilla beans and water. Place onto stove and cook on low heat for 15 minutes. Remove from heat and cool. Strain pineapple and ginger, reserving liquid and vanilla beans. This step can be done the day before. Mix pineapple and ginger mixture with ricotta and set aside.

To serve, place a spoonful of ricotta mixture on each crêpe and fold. Place 2 crêpes on each plate, spooning more pineapple and ricotta mixture on top of each crêpe. Garnish with vanilla bean and drizzle with the reserved syrup.

ricotta cake with poached peach

Makes 1 loaf (8 portions)

Ricotta Cake
1 kg (2 lb) ricotta cheese
50 g (1½ oz) plain flour
125 g (4 oz) sugar
50 ml (1½ fl oz) lemon juice
zest of 1 lemon
6 eggs

Poached Peaches
400 ml (14 fl oz) water
400 g (14 oz) sugar
½ vanilla bean
1 cinnamon quill
200 g (7 oz) dried apricots
4 peaches

To make ricotta cake, preheat oven to 90°C. Grease and line a loaf tin.

Beat the cheese with the flour and sugar. Add the lemon juice, zest and the eggs, one at a time.

Pour mixture into the prepared tin and bake for 90 minutes.

To make poached peaches, bring the water, sugar, vanilla bean and cinnamon quill to the boil. Add the dried apricots.

Slip the skin off the peaches and remove the stone by scooping with a teaspoon from the base.

Reduce liquid to a simmer and poach peaches until cooked. Cool and drain, reserving liquid.

To serve, place a slice of ricotta cake on serving plate and add a poached peach. Top with a spoonful of cooking liquid.

coconut rice pudding with citrus salad

Serves 4

Coconut Rice Pudding

1/2 cinnamon stick

1/2 vanilla bean

1 piece of nutmeg

1 tbsp fresh ginger, chopped

1 litre (4 cups) milk

250 g (8 oz) arborio rice

125 g (4 oz) sugar

400 ml (13 fl oz) tin coconut cream

Citrus Salad

1 lime

1 orange

1 grapefruit

1 tangelo

To make coconut rice pudding, tie up the spices in muslin and add to milk and rice.

Bring to a slow simmer in a heavy-based saucepan, stirring occasionally.

Cook until the rice is completely cooked and the mixture looks like porridge. This will take at least 40 minutes.

In a separate pan, bring the sugar and coconut cream to the boil.

Add to the rice mixture and set aside to cool.

To make citrus salad, peel and segment fruits and gently mix together.

To serve, place coconut rice pudding in bowl and top with segments of citrus fruits.

raspberry muffins

Makes 8 muffins

220 g (7 1/2 oz) butter

2 eggs

170 g (6 oz) sugar

2 tsp baking powder

pinch of salt

160 g (5 1/2 oz) flour

80 ml (1/3 cup) milk

1 punnet of raspberries

icing sugar

Preheat oven to 200°C.

Melt the butter and cool. Whisk the eggs and sugar until thick. Add the butter, sifted dry ingredients and finally the milk. Mix lightly until just combined — do not over mix.

Fold in the raspberries, reserving 8 to place on the top of the muffins. Spoon mixture into muffin paper cases until half full and top each muffin with a reserved raspberry.

Bake for 30 minutes or until golden brown and cooked through.

Dust with icing sugar and serve warm with butter.

baked beans with smoked ham hock

My father used to bake this dish in the hot sand after cooking the fish that he had caught during the day.

Serves 8

750 g (1½ lb) cannellini beans

1 tbsp dry mustard powder

1 medium-sized ham hock

500 ml (2 cups) tomato ketchup

2 medium-sized onions, sliced

80 ml (⅓ cup) treacle

125 g (4 oz) brown sugar

2 bay leaves

Soak beans in 2½ litres (10 cups) water overnight. Drain and rinse under cold water.

In a large, heavy-based saucepan, cover the beans with 2.5 cm salted water. Bring to the boil and skim the beans. Reduce the heat and cook the beans until the skins begin to split. This should take approximately 10 minutes. Drain the beans and reserve the liquid.

Add remaining ingredients and enough of the reserved liquid to cover the beans by 2.5 cm and cover with a tight-fitting lid. Cook in preheated oven at 120°C for at least 8 hours or overnight. When cooked, the beans should appear rich and shiny but not too thick.

Remove the hock from the beans and strip the skin and bone from the meat. Shred the ham and combine it with the finished beans, then serve.

This dish can also be cooked over an open fire or in a camp oven.

Bathers' fruit mocktail

Serves 1

Raspberry Gear
3 tbsp frozen raspberries
45 ml (1 1/2 fl oz) elderflower
   cordial

Fruit Mocktail
1 mango cheek
90 ml (3 fl oz) pineapple juice
4 mint leaves

To make raspberry gear, blend raspberries and cordial until smooth.

To make fruit mocktail, blend mango, pineapple juice and mint with a scoop of ice.

Pour 1 tablespoon raspberry gear into the bottom of a martini glass and top with fruit mocktail.

homemade lemonade

Serves 1

45 ml (1 1/2 fl oz) homemade lemonade
   cordial (see recipe below)
ice
water or soda water

In a 375-ml (1 1/2-cup) tumbler glass, pour homemade lemon cordial over ice and fill with either still water or soda water.

homemade lemonade cordial

Makes approximately 500 ml (2 cups)

400 g (13 oz) sugar
330 ml (11 fl oz) lemon juice
1 lemon, sliced
2 lime leaves

Make cordial by boiling the sugar and juice together. Add lemon and lime leaves and seal in an airtight jar to cool. Store in the fridge for up to 1 week.

cranberry cocktail

Serves 1

crushed ice
1/2 lime
1/2 cup cranberry juice
1/2 cup watermelon juice
1/2 cup pineapple juice

Place crushed ice in glass and squeeze lime juice over it.

Add the other juices and serve immediately.

Balmoral sunrise

Serves 1

500 ml (2 cups) orange juice
juice of 1 lime
1 tsp honey
2 eggs
nutmeg to garnish

Blend all ingredients together to achieve a nice froth. Pour into glasses, and top with freshly grated nutmeg. Serve immediately.

Noon at Bathers'

is watching people stroll along the promenade or

picnicking in the park, the sound of children playing

in the rotunda, a refreshing sea breeze through open

doors, flavours of summer salads or wood-fired pizzas

in winter, a glass of wine, the joy of relaxing with friends

or colleagues and stretching lunch into evening ...

summer salad with baby beetroot

Serves 4

8 baby beetroot

12 yellow baby beetroot

36 broad beans

4 garlic cloves, sliced

6 shallots, peeled and sliced

1 tbsp virgin olive oil

zest of a preserved lemon
   (see recipe page 200)

80 ml ($\frac{1}{3}$ cup) extra virgin olive oil

50 ml ($1\frac{1}{2}$ fl oz) balsamic vinegar

salt and pepper

12 basil leaves

12 yellow teardrop tomatoes, halved

Boil baby beetroot in a separate saucepan for each colour. Cook until tender, cool in liquid, then peel. Leave to one side.

Peel and boil broad beans, then cool in cold water. Strain and leave to one side with beetroot.

Place sliced garlic and shallots in saucepan and sweat them in virgin olive oil. Add strips of preserved lemon zest. Remove from stove and allow to cool. Add extra virgin olive oil and balsamic vinegar and season with salt and pepper.

Place beetroot, beans, basil and tomatoes in a large salad bowl. Toss with dressing, then serve.

chicken salad with celeriac and avocado

Serves 4

1 bulb celeriac

1 leek, peeled, chopped and washed

1 carrot, peeled and chopped

1 onion, peeled and chopped

1 bay leaf

1 sprig fresh sage

1 tsp salt

10 peppercorns

1 chicken, 1.2 kg (2 lb 7 oz)

100 ml (3½ fl oz) sour cream or
   crème fraîche

salt and pepper

2 large avocados, diced

1 head baby cos lettuce, washed and
   separated

Peel celeriac and cut into very fine strips. Keep the peelings for the chicken stock.

Place the leek, carrot, celeriac peelings, onion, herbs, salt and peppercorns in a large pot and cover with cold water. Bring to the boil and simmer for 5 minutes and then add the chicken. Bring back to a gentle simmer and cook for another 5 minutes. Remove from heat, cover, and let rest for 1 hour.

When chicken is at room temperature, drain the stock off the chicken and set aside. Skin the chicken, remove the meat from the bones and tear into small pieces.

Strain the stock through a fine sieve. Take ½ cup cold chicken stock and mix with the sour cream or crème fraîche. Season with salt and pepper. Mix chicken pieces with celeriac strips, avocado dice and creamy dressing.

Place cos lettuce into serving bowl, top with chicken salad and serve.

tomato salad

Serves 4

6 truss tomatoes

12 vine-ripened cherry tomatoes, halved

12 yellow teardrop tomatoes, halved

1 garlic clove, peeled and crushed

50 ml (1 ½ fl oz) white wine vinegar

125 ml (½ cup) extra virgin olive oil

handful of flat leaf parsley leaves

handful of baby basil leaves

freshly milled black pepper

pinch of sea salt

Blanch truss tomatoes in boiling water, then place in cold water for 1 minute. Peel skin off. Cut into wedges.

Place all the tomatoes in a mixing bowl with the garlic, vinegar, olive oil, parsley and basil.

Toss lightly, season with pepper and sea salt, then serve.

asparagus salad, red endive and crème fraîche

Serves 4

1 garlic clove, peeled and finely
  chopped
2 shallots, peeled and finely chopped
150 ml (5 fl oz) vegetable stock
  (see recipe page 193)
100 ml (3½ fl oz) verjuice
200 g (7 oz) crème fraîche
salt and milled black pepper
16 stalks of white asparagus
12 stalks of green asparagus
4 red endive, leaves separated
1–2 tbsp olive oil

Place garlic and shallots in a small saucepan with vegetable stock and verjuice. Bring to a simmer and reduce by a third.

Remove from heat and allow to cool. When cooled, whisk together with crème fraîche, season to taste with salt and pepper and leave to one side.

Peel and blanch asparagus until tender in salted boiling water. Refresh in iced water then remove and dry with paper towel.

Toss asparagus and red endive with the olive oil and season with salt.

Arrange asparagus and endive on serving plate and drizzle with crème fraîche dressing.

goat's cheese tart with tomato salad

Serves 6

Goat's Cheese Tart

50 ml (1 1/2 fl oz) olive oil

8 Spanish onions, sliced

2 pinches of white sugar

2 pinches of thyme leaves

200 g (7 oz) shortcrust pastry
   (see recipe page 197)

350 g (11 oz) goat's cheese

75 ml (2 1/2 fl oz) milk

75 ml (2 1/2 fl oz) cream

3 eggs

salt and pepper

a pinch of paprika

ground nutmeg to taste

Tomato Salad

4 peeled vine-ripened tomatoes,
   quartered

2 beefsteak or similar type of
   tomatoes, quartered

1 punnet of yellow teardrop
tomatoes, halved

1 punnet of cherry tomatoes, halved

2 tbsp extra virgin olive oil

5–6 small basil leaves

sea salt

fresh cracked black pepper

To make goat's cheese tart, preheat oven to 190°C.

In medium pan, heat olive oil. Add onions and sugar and continually stir until brown and very sweet to taste. Add thyme leaves. Stir and then remove from heat and leave to cool.

Line a 26 cm tart shell with pastry rolled out 2 mm thick. Half fill pastry shell with caramelised onions and top with slices of fresh goat's cheese.

Combine milk, cream, eggs, salt and pepper, paprika and ground nutmeg and mix well. Pour over the top of the tart.

Bake in oven until the base of the tart is golden brown and the mixture has set. Cool on a metal rack. Slice the tart with a serrated knife.

To make salad, just toss all of the ingredients together.

To serve, warm up tart gently in the oven. Place on serving plate and cover with tomato salad. Drizzle a little of the olive oil around the plate and finish off with some cracked pepper.

octopus salad with harissa bread

Serves 6

Octopus

500 g (1 lb) large octopus

4 litres (16 cups) water

250 ml (1 cup) red wine

1 onion, sliced

1 tbsp oregano

Salad

200 g (7 oz) tomatoes

300 g (10 oz) red, yellow
    and green capsicums

1 large onion

20 capers

1 preserved lemon
    (see recipe page 200)

1 apple

150 g (5 oz) cucumbers

50 g (1½ oz) black & green olives

salt

2 tbsp chopped coriander

2 tbsp chopped mint

50 ml (1½ fl oz) olive oil

juice of 1 lemon

Harissa Bread

250 ml (1 cup) water

50 ml (1½ fl oz) red wine vinegar

1 tbsp harissa

4 slices of baguette, cut on the
    diagonal

1 preserved lemon
    (see recipe page 200)

To braise the octopus, first trim the head and beak and discard. Cook the leg section in a stock made from water, red wine, onion and oregano for approximately 3 hours or until quite tender. Allow to cool in the liquid and then cut into small chunks and reserve.

To make salad, dice the vegetables into small cubes, season with salt, and mix together with coriander, mint, olive oil and lemon juice.

To make harissa bread, combine the water, vinegar and harissa, and soak the bread in this mixture.

To serve, place the bread on a plate, set the octopus on top and then the salad. Finish with a spoonful of the harissa mix and julienne of preserved lemon.

antipasto with eggplant and capsicum

Serves 4

1 eggplant

salt

olive oil

2 globe artichokes

1 red capsicum

400 g (13 oz) goat's cheese
  and/or fetta cheese

8 basil leaves

12 Kalamata black olives

12 yellow teardrop tomatoes

12 cherry tomatoes

4 sage leaves

80 ml (2½ fl oz) balsamic vinegar

150 ml (5 fl oz) extra virgin
  olive oil

sea salt and black pepper

Cut eggplant lengthways into four slices 2 cm thick. Sprinkle both sides with salt, then allow to stand for 1 hour to draw out the bitter juices.

Wash and dry eggplant, then brush with some olive oil and panfry until golden brown. Remove from pan and set aside to cool.

Peel and blanch artichokes for 3–5 minutes in salted boiling water with a little lemon juice (this will reduce discolouration of artichokes). When cooked but still firm, remove and allow to cool.

Cut capsicum into quarters lengthways and deseed. Brush with olive oil and place on oven tray. Roast in oven at 180°C until scorched and soft. Remove and cool then peel the skin off.

Take an eggplant slice and place a spoonful of goat's cheese (or fetta cheese) into the middle and roll up. Repeat with other slices.

Place roast capsicum on serving plate, top with eggplant roll and artichoke half.

Toss basil leaves, olives, tomatoes and sage leaves with balsamic vinegar and olive oil, sprinkle with sea salt and pepper. Serve on plate with capsicum, eggplant roll and artichoke.

roast scallops with sauce vierge

Serves 4

Sauce Vierge
2 tbsp olive oil
8 shallots, peeled and finely sliced
6 garlic cloves, peeled and finely sliced
1 punnet of cherry tomatoes, halved
handful of flatleaf parsley
handful of basil
handful of baby spinach
50 ml (1$\frac{1}{2}$ fl oz) white wine vinegar
juice of 2 lemons
150 ml (5 fl oz) olive oil
salt and black pepper

24 bay scallops with roe, in shell
100 g (3$\frac{1}{2}$ oz) butter

To make sauce vierge, heat 2 tablespoons olive oil in a pan and add shallots and garlic. Fry until lightly cooked. Add cherry tomatoes and stir until tomatoes are soft. Remove pan from stove and cool.

Finely chop parsley, basil and baby spinach, then add to pan with vinegar, lemon juice and remaining olive oil. Season with salt and milled black pepper and reserve dressing to one side.

To roast scallops, preheat oven to 180°C. Place scallops in baking dish and divide butter into small pieces on top of each scallop. Season with salt. Bake in preheated oven for about 10 minutes.

To serve, place scallops on serving plate, top with a spoonful of sauce vierge and serve.

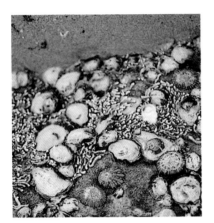

mussels with garlic and cream

Serves 4

3 kg (6 lb) mussels, scrubbed
and debearded
1 tbsp garlic, peeled and chopped
125 ml (½ cup) white wine
300 ml (10 fl oz) cream
1 tbsp chopped flatleaf parsley

Heat a large pan until it is very hot. Add the mussels, then the garlic and wine. Allow the mussels to steam under a lid until they open. (**Note:** it is important to retain the heat in the pan so do not add too much liquid, just enough to create steam — the mussels already contain a lot of water.)

After 3 minutes discard the mussels that have not opened.

Add the cream and allow the mussels to simmer in the soup until the sauce is slightly thickened. Place in large bowl and garnish with parsley.

Serve with homemade chips and a small salad.

little bites of prawns, cuttlefish, olive balls and chilli relish

Serves 4

200 g (7 oz) arborio rice

400 ml (13 fl oz) fish stock
   (see recipe page 192)

150 g (5 oz) Kalamata olives,
   deseeded

zest of 1 preserved lemon
   (see recipe page 200)

100 g (3½ oz) white scallop meat

2 pinches of dill leaves

2 baby cuttlefish, cleaned and cut
   into 8 pieces

4 baby red mullet, filleted and boned

12 green tiger prawns, deveined

flour for dusting

1 quantity of saffron batter
   (see recipe page 33)

salt for seasoning

oil for deep-frying

1 quantity of chilli relish
   (see recipe page 196)

handful of baby watercress salad

In a large saucepan place rice and fish stock and bring to the boil. Cover and reduce heat to a simmer and cook until all the fish stock has been absorbed, approximately 15–20 minutes. Set aside to cool.

In a food processor, process olives with lemon zest, scallop meat and dill leaves. Blend quickly to small pieces.

Remove olive mixture from food processor and combine in a bowl with cooked rice. Roll tablespoons full of mixture into small olive-shaped balls. Place on a tray in refrigerator until needed.

Dust seafood with flour, then 1 at a time dip in batter and deep-fry in hot oil until golden and cooked. Remove and drain on paper towel. Repeat with each piece until all seafood is cooked.

While oil is still hot, fry 2 olive balls at a time until golden brown. Remove and drain on paper towel. Season seafood and olive balls with salt.

Serve seafood and olive balls hot with chilli relish and tossed baby watercress salad.

roast mushrooms with gorgonzola, polenta and baby spinach

Serves 4

4 jumbo flat field mushrooms

2 garlic cloves, peeled and crushed

2 pinches of thyme leaves

150 ml (5 oz) olive oil

4 shallots, peeled and chopped

200 ml (7 fl oz) vegetable stock
   (see recipe page 193)

50 g (1½ oz) instant polenta

salt and pepper

80 g (3 oz) crumbled gorgonzola
   cheese

4 handfuls of baby spinach, sautéed

cracked black pepper to serve

1 punnet of enoki or chestnut
   mushrooms (optional)

Preheat oven to 140°C.

Peel and core field mushrooms, place in ovenproof dish and sprinkle with the crushed garlic and thyme. Set aside 2 tablespoons of the olive oil, then drizzle the rest over the mushrooms, crushed garlic and thyme. Roast mushrooms for 30 minutes, then remove from oven and cool.

In a small saucepan, heat remaining olive oil then sweat shallots. Add vegetable stock and bring to a simmer. Add polenta, lower heat and stir until smooth, about 15 minutes. Season with salt and pepper. Remove from stove, add gorgonzola cheese and stir until melted.

Reheat mushrooms, then place on serving plates and top with polenta, sautéed baby spinach and cracked black pepper. If using the other mushrooms as well, sauté them and add to the topping.

cassolette of clams, vongole and pippies

Serves 6

6 vine-ripened tomatoes

24 surf clams

36 vongole

36 pippies

4 shallots, peeled and finely chopped

2 garlic cloves, peeled and finely chopped

150 ml (5 fl oz) white wine

100 ml (3½ fl oz) fish stock (see recipe page 192)

100 g (3½ oz) unsalted butter

1 bunch of parsley, finely chopped

1 bunch of chervil, finely chopped

Plunge the tomatoes into boiling water for 3 seconds and then straight into iced water. Peel them, cut into quarters, remove the seeds and cut into 5 mm dice.

Rinse the molluscs in cold water to remove any grit from the shells and drain. Heat a heavy-based pot with a matching lid on the stove until it is very hot.

Mix the shallots and garlic through the molluscs and add enough to the pot to cover the bottom of the pot. Quickly add the wine and fish stock and cover. Cook for about 3 minutes, shaking the pot occasionally.

When the shells are open add some of the butter, herbs and tomato dice and mix through. Discard any molluscs whose shells have not opened.

Serve immediately.

cauliflower soup with white beans and fontina

Serves 4

200 g (7 oz) white beans
(cannellini beans)

1 medium-sized cauliflower

50 ml (1 ½ fl oz) olive oil

1 small onion, chopped

4 garlic cloves, peeled and crushed

1 bay leaf

½ tsp cayenne pepper

1.5 litres (6 cups) vegetable stock
(see recipe page 193)

200 ml (7 fl oz) fresh cream

sea salt and white pepper

400 g (13 oz) fontina cheese,
shredded

Soak beans in water overnight. Drain and discard liquid.

Remove and discard outside leaves and core of cauliflower. Cut remaining cauliflower into small pieces.

Heat oil in medium-sized saucepan. Add onion and garlic and cook until soft. Add beans, bay leaf, cayenne pepper and stock. Bring to a light simmer and cook slowly for 1 hour. Add the cauliflower and cook for another 30 minutes.

Blend with stick blender, then add cream. Season with salt and white pepper.

Serve soup steaming hot, topped with fontina cheese.

chilli bread

Makes 4 small oval breads

1 ½ tsp dry yeast

pinch sugar

3 tbsp warm milk

1 cup unbleached bakers flour

250 ml (1 cup) hot water

2 tbs olive oil

1 tsp salt

100 g (3 ½ oz) lightly-fried chopped garlic and fresh chillies

1 ½ – 2 cups unbleached bakers flour

Combine yeast, sugar, milk, 1 cup flour and water in large bowl. Beat well with a whisk until smooth and creamy. Cover with a tea towel and let rise at room temperature for 15–30 minutes, or until bubbly.

Add half of the oil and salt, 50 g (1 ½ oz) of the chilli and garlic mixture, and 1 cup of remaining flour to sponge mixture. Whisk hard for about 3 minutes, or until smooth. Continue adding flour (½ cup at a time) with a wooden spoon, until a soft, sticky dough is formed.

Turn dough out on a lightly-floured surface and knead, adding 1 tbsp flour at a time as needed to make a soft, smooth dough. Be careful not to add too much flour or the dough will become too dry.

Divide dough into 4 and shape each quarter into oval-shaped balls. Baste with remaining oil and garlic and chilli mixture, cover and let rest for 60 minutes in a warm place.

Preheat oven to 180°C. Bake rolls for 25–30 minutes or until crisp and brown. Remove and let cool on wire racks.

fougasse pizza with cabicou and dried ratatouille

Serves 4

1 small zucchini

1 baby eggplant

1 small red capsicum

1 small yellow capsicum

1 brown onion, peeled

100 ml (3 1/2 fl oz) olive oil

4 garlic cloves, peeled and sliced

1 punnet of cherry tomatoes, halved

4 oval-shaped pizza bases
   (see recipe page 196)

4 large desiree potatoes, peeled
   and sliced wafer-thin

2 tsp thyme leaves

2 large handfuls of wild rocket

200 g (7 oz) crumbled fresh
   cabicou cheese

sea salt

freshly milled black pepper

Preheat oven to maximum temperature.

Dice the zucchini, eggplant, red capsicum, yellow capsicum and brown onion into 2 cm cubes.

Heat half the olive oil in frying pan and then add the onions and cook for 3 minutes. Add the garlic, zucchini, eggplant and capsicum and sauté at high heat until lightly cooked. Remove from heat and then add the cherry tomatoes. Leave to one side.

Brush some of the remaining olive oil on the pizza bases. Arrange sliced potatoes on top of bases, sprinkle with thyme leaves and then brush with remaining olive oil and some sea salt. Cook in oven for 10 minutes or until lightly brown, then place ratatouille vegetables on top. Return pizzas to oven and cook until base is golden, about another 3 minutes.

Remove pizzas from oven and place on serving plates. Toss wild rocket with cabicou cheese and the rest of the olive oil and sprinkle on top of pizza. Season with sea salt and freshly milled black pepper.

smoked salmon, fennel and mascarpone pizza

Serves 4

1 quantity of pizza dough
   (see recipe page 196)
1 cup of homemade tomato pizza
   sauce (see recipe page 194)
1 cup of grated mozzarella cheese
300 g (10 oz) smoked salmon
1 fennel bulb, shaved, soaked in
   cold water and drained
handful of English spinach leaves
6 tbsp mascarpone cheese

Preheat oven to maximum. Roll out pizza dough very thinly and spread with tomato sauce. Top with mozzarella.

Bake on an unglazed stone tile or a pizza tray until pizza is golden brown, approximately 10 minutes.

Garnish the hot pizza with smoked salmon, shaved fennel, fresh spinach leaves and mascarpone cheese and serve immediately.

chestnut soup

Serves 6

750 g (1 ½ lb) chestnuts
olive oil
5 shallots, peeled
3 garlic cloves, peeled
2 litres (8 cups) chicken stock
   (see recipe page 192)
1 tbsp butter
100 ml (3 ½ fl oz) cream
sea salt and white pepper

Preheat oven to 220°C. Score the chestnuts with a paring knife all the way around the diameter — be very careful! Lightly rub with olive oil and place on a baking tray. Roast in a hot oven until the chestnuts start to split open, approximately 5–7 minutes.

Peel the chestnuts while they are still hot as they are much easier to peel, but you might need to use gloves. Roughly slice the roasted chestnuts, shallots and garlic cloves.

In a medium-sized pot add the butter. Gently sweat off the shallots, garlic and chestnuts without colouring. Add the chicken stock and bring to a simmer. Cook until all ingredients are soft, about 1 hour.

Drain the excess cooking liquor and reserve. Purée chestnut mixture in a blender, adding the reserved cooking liquor until the required consistency is achieved. Stir in the cream and reheat gently. Adjust the seasoning with a little sea salt and white milled pepper.

Serving suggestions: this dish can be served with duck foie gras, duck confit and wilted spinach or with sautéed Jerusalem artichokes and a few thyme leaves.

maccheroni pasta with pork bolognaise

Serves 4

500 g (1 lb) fresh Italian fennel
    and pork sausages
150 ml (5 fl oz) olive oil
2 brown onions, peeled and
    finely chopped
4 garlic cloves, peeled and
    finely chopped
1 tsp fennel seeds, roasted
    and ground
90 g (3 oz) tomato paste
1 glass red wine
12-16 very ripe roma tomatoes,
    skinned and roughly chopped
2 bay leaves
salt and pepper
handful of fresh chopped flatleaf
    parsley
handful of fresh chopped oregano
450 g (15 oz) maccheroni
    (macaroni) pasta
butter
freshly shaved parmesan cheese

Split the skins of the sausages and remove the meat. Heat olive oil in medium-sized saucepan, add onions and fry over medium heat until they are golden and caramelised. Add garlic and ground fennel and stir through, then add the sausage meat and fry until almost all the liquid has evaporated. Cook until meat starts to crumble — it is very important to break up the meat during this stage to avoid having large chunks of pale meat.

Stir in the tomato paste and cook until it begins to catch on the pan. Deglaze the pan with the red wine and add the fresh tomato. Bring to the boil then reduce to a gentle simmer. Add the bay leaves and season with salt and pepper, then cook very slowly for 1–1½ hours to bring the flavours together and soften the meat. The meat should be soft and the sauce rich and thick. Correct the seasoning and add the fresh herbs.

Bring large pan of salted water to the boil. Cook pasta until al denté, then drain and toss in a little butter. Season with salt and pepper. Divide hot drained pasta between serving plates and top with sauce and freshly shaved parmesan cheese.

sweet onion and goat's cheese ricotta ravioli with thyme burnt butter

Serves 4

Pasta Dough

300 g (10 oz) plain flour

1 pinch salt

3 eggs

1 tbsp olive oil

50 ml (1½ fl oz) chlorophyll
   (see recipe page 193)

For the Ravioli

4 medium onions

50 ml (1½ fl oz) olive oil

200 g (7 oz) goat's cheese ricotta

pepper

2 sprigs thyme, diced

egg wash

150 g (5 oz) cold butter

To make pasta dough, combine the flour and salt. On a workbench, form a mound with the salted flour and make a well in the centre. In a bowl mix the eggs, olive oil and chlorophyll. Pour the egg mixture into the centre of the flour and slowly incorporate the flour with your hands, a little at a time, until you form a firm dough.

Clean the bench with a scraper, incorporating the scrapings into the dough and, after dusting the bench with flour, knead the dough with the heel of your hand for 10 minutes or until it is smooth.

Wrap in plastic wrap and refrigerate for 1 hour.

Divide the dough into 3 portions. Lightly dust a bench with some flour and roll each portion of dough through a pasta machine or with a rolling pin until 1–2 mm thick. Dust lightly with flour. Using a fluted ravioli cutter, cut each portion of dough into 8, making 7 cm squares. Stack in a small pile and wrap with plastic wrap until ready to use.

To make ravioli, peel the onions, then cut in half and slice finely to achieve even

strands. In a heavy pan, warm the oil and sweat the onions very slowly for 30 minutes or until they are an even, golden colour. Drain and allow to cool. When cold, add half the ricotta, some pepper and half the thyme leaves.

Place a teaspoonful of filling in the centre of half of the sheets of pre-prepared ravioli pasta. Brush the sides with the egg wash and cover with another ravioli sheet, pressing all the edges to seal well. Trim with a ravioli cutter. Cover and refrigerate for 30 minutes.

To make the burnt butter, heat all but 1 teaspoon of the butter in a small frying pan. Once the butter finishes frothing, it will start to turn a hazelnut colour; remove it immediately from the heat and then add the rest of the butter and the remaining thyme leaves.

To serve, plunge all the ravioli into a large pot of boiling salted water. Cook for 3 minutes, drain, then spoon onto a warm plate and place the remaining ricotta on top of each ravioli.

Pour the burnt butter over the ravioli and serve at once.

bavette with squid, prawns, garlic and chilli

Serves 4

250 g (8 oz) bavette pasta
50 ml (1½ fl oz) olive oil
8 shallots, peeled and sliced
4 garlic cloves, peeled and chopped
2 large red chillies, finely sliced
8 baby squid tubes, sliced
8 baby prawns, peeled
100 g (3½ oz) butter
juice of 1 lemon
salt and pepper

Bring a large pot of salted water to the boil and cook pasta until it is just done. Drain and keep warm.

While pasta is cooking, heat olive oil in a frying pan until hot. Add shallots and cook until golden, then add garlic and sliced chillies and cook for another minute. Add squid and prawns, stir until just cooked, then add warm drained pasta. Toss together and remove from heat.

Add butter and lemon juice and stir through until butter is melted. Divide among serving plates and season with salt and pepper. Serve immediately.

ricotta and spinach panzotti with chunky tomato sauce

Serves 4

4 bunches of English spinach

1 tbsp olive oil

4 garlic cloves, peeled and crushed

4 shallots, peeled and chopped

200 g (7 oz) fresh ricotta cheese

salt and pepper

1 quantity of pasta dough
   (see recipe page 82)

egg wash

400 ml (13 fl oz) chunky tomato
   sauce (see recipe page 195)

2 tbsp butter

3 tbsp olive oil

Wash spinach then blanch in boiling water. Remove and refresh in cold water, then drain again and place on paper towel to dry. Chop half the spinach roughly.

In a frying pan heat 1 tablespoon olive oil and fry garlic and shallots until lightly done, then add chopped spinach and stir. Remove from heat and allow to cool. Mix with ricotta cheese. Season with salt and pepper.

Roll out pasta dough until it is very thin, (the lowest setting on a pasta machine) then cut into 10 cm squares. Place a spoonful of ricotta and spinach mix into centre of each square, brush edges with egg wash and fold to form a triangle. Press edges together to seal.

Bring a large pan of salted water to the boil and cook pasta until cooked but still firm. Remove from water and drain. Sauté remaining spinach in 1 tablespoon butter and 2 tablespoons olive oil. Set aside.

Heat the remaining butter and olive oil in a frying pan and add pasta. Cook until heated through and lightly browned. Turn over and add 1 tablespoon water to cook further. Remove from pan and place on serving plates. Top with chunky tomato sauce and sautéed whole spinach leaves.

papillote of ocean trout

Serves 6

2 tbsp olive oil

1 Spanish onion, finely sliced

250 ml (1 cup) of stock, chicken or
fish (see recipe page 192)

1 bay leaf

1 sprig of thyme

1 garlic bulb, peeled

8–10 shallots, peeled

250 g (8 oz) butter, softened

bunch of chives, chopped

bunch of flatleaf parsley, chopped

1 preserved lemon, chopped
(see recipe page 200)

1 tbsp butter

12 baby leeks or spring onions,
washed and trimmed

salt and pepper

6 fillets of ocean trout,
180 g (6 oz) per portion

6 pieces of silicon paper

romesco sauce
(see recipe page 195)

6 lemon cheeks to serve

Heat the oil in a saucepan, add the onion and cook slowly until soft.

Add the stock, bay leaf and thyme and cook slowly until all the stock is evaporated, then season. Purée in a food processor and cool completely.

Preheat the oven to 180°C. Wrap the peeled garlic and shallots in a piece of foil and roast them in the oven until very soft. Purée this and reserve.

In a food processor whip the softened butter, add the chives and parsley. Add the preserved lemon rind and season.

Sauté the baby leeks in butter, then let them then cool.

Preheat oven to 250°C. On a circular piece of silicon paper (30 cm diameter) place a spoonful of shallot purée at the base. Place a piece of ocean trout on top of the purée and season. On top of the ocean trout, place the baby leeks, the Spanish onion mixture and a knob of the flavoured butter.

Fold the top half of the paper over and seal the edges by folding around outside of the paper. To cook, place on oven tray and bake in oven for approximately 10 minutes.

Serve immediately (to avoid overcooking) with roasted small potatoes, romesco sauce and a lemon cheek.

seared swordfish fillet with ragout of lentils

Serves 4

Seared Swordfish

50 ml (1½ fl oz) extra virgin olive oil

1 tbsp butter

4 x 160 g (5½ oz) swordfish fillet
   medallions (round-shaped)

60 ml (2 fl oz) olive oil

pepper

Ragout of Lentils

1 garlic clove, peeled and chopped

1 shallot, peeled and chopped

1 carrot

1 stick of celery

1 leek

50 ml (1½ fl oz) olive oil

400 g (13 oz) brown lentils

1 sprig of thyme

1 bay leaf

butter

1 quantity of olive tapenade
   (see recipe page 201)

1 quantity of oven-roasted tomatoes
   (see recipe page 200)

1 quantity of spinach purée
   (see page 199)

1 quantity of capsicum and basil oil
   (see recipe page 202)

To make seared swordfish, pour the olive oil into a hot frying pan and add the butter. When the butter is foamy and gold, sear off the swordfish fillets on both sides until they are medium rare. Drain them, and set aside (season them just before serving, with fresh ground pepper only).

To make ragout of lentils, preheat the oven to 180°C. Cut all the vegetables into a brunoise (small dice) and sweat them in the olive oil until they are cooked.

Add the lentils and herbs and cover with water. Cover with greaseproof paper and braise in the oven until the lentils are tender.

To serve, firstly season the swordfish with ground pepper, spread the tapenade over one side, place the oven-roasted tomatoes over the tapenade and finish cooking in the oven until the fish is medium (approximately 6 minutes).

Warm up the lentil ragout, stir in a nut of butter, and season with salt and pepper.

Warm up the spinach purée and season with salt and pepper.

In the centre of a hot plate arrange the lentil ragout into a circle and top with the puréed spinach.

Place the swordfish (with the oven-roasted tomato) on top of the layered lentils and spinach and drizzle with the capsicum and basil oil around the swordfish.

Serve hot.

snapper carpaccio with fennel

Serves 6

Snapper Carpaccio

600 g (1¼ lb) piece of snapper fillet,
   skin removed

olive oil

sea salt

white pepper

Salad

2 handfuls of small leaves
   (baby cress or rocket)

1 large fennel bulb, shaved

50 ml (1½ fl oz) extra virgin olive oil

lemon oil (optional)

To make snapper carpaccio, trim the snapper of any dark, oily parts.

Cut widthwise into 4 pieces. Slice the flesh side of the fillet nearly in two, like a butterfly.

Place a sheet of plastic wrap on a heavy cutting board, brush with a touch of olive oil. Place snapper on prepared wrap, brush the top with a little oil, cover with another sheet of plastic wrap and, using a wooden mallet or heavy pan, gently pound each piece of snapper until you have a large circular piece. Put the snapper aside on a plate. Repeat with the remainder of the snapper pieces.

To serve, place the snapper on a plate, sprinkle with sea salt and some milled white pepper. Set the salad leaves and the shaved fennel on top of the snapper and drizzle with the olive oil and the lemon oil if you have some. Alternatively, you could squeeze the juice of one lemon over the snapper 5 minutes before you serve it and finish with some extra virgin olive oil.

roast duck with fresh nectarines on potato cake

Serves 4

Roast Duck

3 litres (12 cups) water

500 ml (2 cups) white vinegar

2 whole white ducks

4 fresh oranges, juiced

500 ml (2 cups) soy sauce

200 g (7 oz) brown sugar

1 pinch of ground cinnamon

50 g (1½ oz) ginger, chopped

50 g (1½ oz) garlic, peeled and
   chopped

Potato Cake

4 large pontiac potatoes

salt and pepper

50 g (1½ oz) flatleaf parsley,
   chopped

6 sage leaves, chopped

100 g (3½ fl oz) melted butter

2 tbsp vegetable oil

4 large fresh ripe nectarines

4 handfuls of fresh watercress,
   lightly blanched

To roast duck, bring water and vinegar to boil in a large saucepan. Place duck into boiling water and vinegar and leave for 5 minutes. Remove duck from saucepan and drain duck for 20 minutes. Again, place duck into boiling water and vinegar for 5 minutes. Drain again and place on oven rack for roasting.

Preheat oven to 140°C. In a small pot, simmer over low heat the orange juice, soy sauce, sugar, cinnamon, ginger and garlic until thick. Brush this mixture with a pastry brush onto the skin of the duck and allow to dry. Repeat this step.

Place duck into preheated oven and roast until duck is cooked, approximately 1½ hours. When cooked, remove from oven and set aside to cool.

To make potato cake, peel and wash potatoes. Shred finely and mix with salt and pepper, parsley, sage and a little of the melted butter. Form this mixture into 4 medium-sized cakes, then sauté each in a nonstick frying pan until cooked and golden with some oil and the rest of the melted butter. Remove and place on serving plates.

To serve, cut nectarines into wedges. Remove meat from the bones of the duck and cut into small pieces. Place duck meat and nectarine wedges on potato cakes then top with blanched watercress and serve.

turkey scaloppine with eggplant polenta

Serves 4

4 bunches of English spinach

1 medium eggplant

2 tbsp olive oil

100 ml (3½ fl oz) olive oil

4 shallots, peeled and chopped

4 garlic cloves, peeled and chopped

200 ml (7 fl oz) chicken stock
  (see recipe page 192)

200 g (7 oz) instant polenta

100 g (3½ oz) butter

salt and milled black pepper

4 turkey fillets, 170 g (6 oz) each,
  flattened

1 tbsp butter

1 tbsp oil

1 tbsp butter (for sautéing spinach)

400 ml (13 fl oz) chunky tomato
  sauce (see recipe page 195)

Trim stalks from spinach and wash. Blanch spinach in boiling salted water then remove and refresh in cold water. Drain on paper towel until needed.

Slice eggplant lengthways 3 mm thick. Heat 2 tablespoons olive oil in a frying pan, soften each side of the eggplant then reserve.

In a medium saucepan, heat remaining olive oil and add shallots and garlic. Sweat shallots and garlic, then add chicken stock and salt to taste. Bring to simmer then add polenta and stir until thick and smooth. Place into a buttered rectangular dish, 10 x 20 cm diameter and approximately 4 cm deep. Allow to cool, then refrigerate until polenta is cold and set.

Preheat oven to 140°C. Cut polenta into large baton-shaped pieces. Lay the eggplant on a bench, slightly overlapping each other. Set the polenta on top at one end and roll over to cover all the polenta. Place butter into an ovenproof dish and then add polenta and eggplant and bake for 15 minutes.

In a frying pan sauté turkey in butter and oil until cooked, then place on serving plate with polenta and eggplant.

Sauté spinach with butter and seasoning, drain and then place on top of eggplant polenta and serve with chunky tomato sauce.

veal scaloppine with lemon and broccolini

Serves 4

8 veal scaloppine, flattened,
  approximately 90 g (3 oz) each
plain flour for dusting veal
100 ml (3½ fl oz) olive oil
1 garlic clove, peeled and crushed
juice of 2 lemons
150 g (5 oz) butter
salt and pepper
4 bunches of broccolini, blanched

Dust each piece of veal with flour. Heat olive oil in frying pan and add veal, sautéing on low heat until cooked, with no colour. Set aside and keep warm.

Add garlic, sautéing until golden. Add lemon juice and butter and stir until melted. Season with salt and pepper.

Place veal on serving plate, top with broccolini and sauce and then serve at once.

seared skirt steak with shallots

Serves 4

50 ml (1½ fl oz) vegetable oil

4 pieces skirt steak, 180 g (6 oz) each

100 g (3½ oz) butter

8 shallots

2 glasses of red wine (preferably shiraz)

2 sprigs of fresh tarragon

salt and pepper

In a very hot pan add the oil then a touch of butter. Sear the seasoned steak and cook at a high heat for 1–2 minutes on each side.

Remove from the pan, add the shallots and some more butter. Cook the shallots until they are soft (about 3 minutes) then add the red wine. Cook down until the wine is reduced by half. Add the remaining butter and stir in. Add the tarragon.

To serve, place the steak on a warm plate and drizzle with the sauce. Season to taste with salt and pepper.

stuffed baby chicken

Serves 1

Stuffing

1 onion, diced

1 rasher of bacon, diced

2 big field mushrooms, diced and fried

50 g (1½ oz) of butter

½ a loaf of stale bread, diced

1 bunch of sage, torn

½ a bunch of parsley, chopped

Chicken

1 small chicken, 500–600 g (16–19 oz)

salt and pepper

1 garlic bulb, broken but not peeled

20 olives

1 lemon, topped and tailed and
    sliced in four

extra virgin olive oil

250 ml (1 cup) chicken stock

50 ml (1 ½ fl oz) verjuice

To make the stuffing, fry the onion, bacon and mushroom in the butter. Add the bread, the sage and the parsley and mix well to combine all ingredients.

To roast the chicken, preheat oven to 180°C. Clean and rinse the chicken and pat dry. Sprinkle with salt and pepper inside and out.

Place the stuffing inside the cavity and truss the chicken or simply tie the legs together. Take an oven tray and place the garlic cloves, olives and the sliced lemons in the base of the pan (this acts as a bed for the chicken). Place the chicken in the pan and brush with oil.

Place the chicken in oven for 15 minutes. Remove from oven and baste the chicken with pan juices, then return to oven and cook for a further 15 minutes at 165°C. Finally, turn the chicken over and cook for 5 more minutes.

Remove the chicken, the garlic, olives and the lemon from the oven and place it on a plate to rest.

Remove the excess fat from the pan and add the chicken stock and verjuice. Remove the chicken meat from the bone, reserve the stuffing and place the bones in with the stock. Reduce the liquid by two thirds and strain.

To serve, place the stuffing on the serving plate and place some of the lemon, olives and garlic around the plates. Place the chicken on top of the stuffing and pour the sauce over. Serve.

passionfruit roulade

Makes 1 roulade

Passionfruit Curd

60 g (2 oz) passionfruit pulp,
   strained with seeds reserved

90 g (3 oz) butter

60 g (2 oz) sugar

2 eggs

Sponge

3 eggs

60 g (2 oz) sugar

drop of vanilla essence

50 g (1½ oz) plain flour, sifted

icing sugar for dusting

To make passionfruit curd, bring the pulp and butter to boil in a large saucepan.

Mix together the sugar and eggs and add to the boiling liquids. Whisk continuously until the mixture comes back to the boil.

Pour into a bowl and allow to cool. Add 3 teaspoons of passionfruit seeds.

To make sponge, preheat oven to 240°C. Line a baking tray with greaseproof paper.

Whisk the eggs and sugar until light and fluffy in an electric mixer (this will take about 4 minutes). Add the vanilla essence and fold in the sifted flour.

Spread mixture about 5 mm thick onto the prepared baking tray. Bake for 3–4 minutes, until golden brown.

To serve, when sponge is cool, thinly spread with the curd and roll up. Dust with icing sugar.

lemon meringue tartlets

Makes 6

Sweet Pastry
200 g (7 oz) butter
200 g (7 oz) sugar
2 eggs
400 g (13 oz) flour
pinch of salt
drop of vanilla essence

Lemon Curd
120 ml (4 fl oz) fresh lemon juice
180 g (6 oz) butter
120 g (4 oz) sugar
2 eggs

Meringue
2 egg whites
150 g (5 oz) castor sugar

To make sweet pastry, cream together the butter and sugar. Add the eggs and finally the flour, salt and vanilla. Allow pastry to chill until soft but firm.

Roll out onto a lightly floured surface until 2.5 mm thick. Cut into circles to fit into lightly greased tartlet cases, 9 cm diameter and 2 cm deep.

Allow to firm up in the fridge then prick the pastry all over with a fork to prevent the sides shrinking. Bake in the oven at 190°C until golden brown. Allow to cool.

To make lemon curd, bring the lemon juice and butter to boil in a saucepan. Mix together the sugar and eggs and add to the boiling liquid, whisking continuously until it reboils.

Pour lemon curd into a bowl and allow to cool.

To make meringue peaks, preheat oven to 110°C.

Mix the egg whites and sugar in a bowl and place over a saucepan of boiling water. Whisk occasionally, until the mixture is warm and the sugar has dissolved.

Take off the heat and whisk continuously with an electric hand beater until thick (this will take about 4 minutes).

Pipe the meringue into small peaks onto a baking tray lined with greaseproof paper. Bake for 30–40 minutes.

To serve, fill pastry cases with lemon curd and decorate with the baked meringue peaks. Serve immediately.

chocolate brownies

Makes 36

4 eggs

350 g (11½ oz) dark brown sugar

175 g (6 oz) melted dark chocolate

250 g (8 oz) melted butter

100 g (3½ oz) plain flour

2 tsp baking powder

3 drops vanilla essence

2 tbsp chocolate drops or raisins

Preheat oven to 160°C. Grease and line with greaseproof paper a square baking tray 20 x 20 cm.

Whisk the eggs and sugar together by hand or in a small mixer until the mixture is smooth. Add the melted chocolate and butter and mix well. Sift flour and baking powder together and fold through chocolate mixture. Add the vanilla essence and chocolate drops or raisins.

Pour mixture into prepared tray and bake for 30–40 minutes or until firm to the touch. Let cool in tin and then cut into small squares or fingers.

raspberry and bread puddings

Makes 8

4 eggs

80 g (3 oz) sugar

325 ml (10½ fl oz) cream

325 ml (10½ fl oz) milk

1 tsp vanilla essence

day-old sliced bread, brioche or croissant

1 cup of seasonal berries, raisins or other
    fruit (such as apricots or cherries),
    stoned, peeled and sliced

Preheat oven to 140°C.

Mix the eggs and sugar together until the sugar has dissolved, then add the cream, milk and vanilla essence. Pass mixture through a fine sieve.

Lightly grease 8 dariole moulds, 90 ml capacity, 7 cm high and 5 cm in diameter. In the greased moulds, layer the bread, brioche or croissant with the fruit and pour over the egg mixture to soak well.

Place moulds into a large baking dish, and fill with enough hot water to come halfway up the sides.

Bake for 30 minutes. Serve with icecream or custard.

lemon and passionfruit delicious

Serves 6

a little melted butter, to grease

sugar, to sprinkle

90 g (3 oz) soft butter

300 g (10 oz) sugar

zest of 2 lemons

75 g (2½ oz) plain flour

½ tsp baking powder

80 ml (⅓ cup) warm passionfruit juice

4 eggs, separated

200 ml (1 cup) milk

pinch of salt

Preheat the oven to 180°C. Lightly butter 6 one-cup capacity ramekins (oval shaped, 10 cm long, 6.5 cm wide and 5 cm deep) and sprinkle with sugar.

Cream the butter, sugar and lemon zest. Sift flour and baking powder together.

Add the passionfruit juice and then the egg yolks (alternating with the flour) to the creamed mixture, making sure the bowl is scraped regularly while mixing. Mix in the milk.

Whisk the egg whites with a pinch of salt to a soft peak. Fold through one-third of the egg whites into the mix, then gently fold through the rest of the egg whites.

Divide the mixture between the ramekins. Place ramekins into a large baking dish and fill with enough hot water to come halfway up the sides. Bake in the oven for 1½ hours.

lime crème brûlée

Serves 4

6 egg yolks

100 g (3 oz) sugar

zest of 1 lime

600 ml (20 fl oz) cream

2 drops of lime oil

extra sugar for caramelising

Preheat oven to 100°C.

Whisk together the yolks, sugar and zest. Bring cream to the boil in a small saucepan and then pour over egg mixture and whisk. Add the oil and pass mixture through a fine sieve.

Pour into 200 ml ramekins and bake in a water bath for 30–40 minutes, or until set. Let the custard cool.

To form a nice caramelised crust, a hand blowtorch will give the best result, or you can use a very hot grill. Sprinkle white sugar all over the ramekin and quickly melt the surface with the blowtorch or the preheated grill, until you have a nice golden crust. Serve immediately.

scones

Makes 10

180 g (6 oz) plain flour

1 tsp baking powder

45 g (1 1/2 oz) butter

1 egg

35 g (1 oz) sugar

70 ml (2 fl oz) warm milk

egg wash for glazing scones

Preheat oven to 190°C.

Sift the flour and baking powder together into a bowl and lightly rub in the butter with fingertips until mixture resembles fine breadcrumbs.

Add the egg, followed by the sugar (which has been dissolved in the warm milk). Very gently mix together until just combined.

Roll dough out on a floured surface to about 2 cm thick. Cut out with a scone cutter and place on oven tray. Brush scones with egg wash.

Bake for 15–20 minutes or until golden brown. Serve hot with jam and cream.

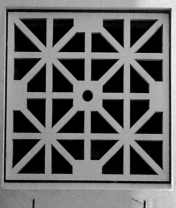

Evening at Bathers'

is seeing the sun setting on the cliffs and sand, having a

drink with friends, enjoying the beautifully crafted dishes

and considered wine list of the restaurant, watching the

moon rising and the seagulls settling in for the night on

the shark net, feeling the warm breeze of a summer night

or smelling the wood burning in the fireplace in winter ...

lime scallop on cucumber

Serves 8

8 white scallops

juice of 2 limes

pinch of grated ginger

50 g (1½ oz) enoki mushrooms,
   cut into small pieces

50 g (1½ oz) Shiitake mushrooms,
   finely sliced

2 dashes mirin (Japanese rice wine)

sea salt

1 telegraph or continental cucumber

8 coriander leaves

Bring scallops to room temperature and place in a bowl with lime juice, ginger, mushrooms, mirin and sea salt. Mix lightly and leave to marinate for 1 hour.

Peel cucumber and cut into disks 1 cm thick. Place on serving plate.

Remove scallops from marinade and place on top of cucumber disks. Strain mushrooms from marinade and place a small amount on top of each scallop.

Top with a coriander leaf and serve.

oysters on cucumber

Makes 12

1 English cucumber
1 lime
salt and white pepper
12 freshly shucked oysters
   (Sydney Rock or Pacific)

Wash the cucumbers in cold water and, using a mandoline, slice them to make a fine julienne. (If you don't have a mandoline you could use a sharp knife to make the julienne.)

In a bowl, marinate the cucumber with the juice of one lime and a touch of salt. Let it stand for 3 minutes and then drain in a colander and pat dry with paper towel.

Season the cucumber with a touch of salt and freshly ground white pepper and place in the empty oyster shells. Top with the oysters and serve on a platter.

goat's cheese gougères

Makes 20 balls

Gougères
125 ml ($\frac{1}{2}$ cup) water
50 g (1$\frac{1}{2}$ oz) butter
a pinch of salt
75 g (2$\frac{1}{2}$ oz) plain flour, sifted
2 eggs
2 tbsp sea salt

Goat's Cheese Filling
400 g (13 oz) fresh goat's curd
1 tbsp thyme leaves, finely chopped

To make gougères, preheat oven to 200°C.

Bring to a boil the water, butter and salt. Add the flour and stir over the heat until the mixture comes away from the sides of the pan.

Take off the heat and transfer to a bowl. Beat for 2–3 minutes until warm, not hot, gradually adding the eggs and mixing in fully until a dropping consistency is acquired.

Pipe gougères the size of 10-cent coins onto a greased baking tray, sprinkle with sea salt flakes and bake until golden brown.

To serve, mix the goat's cheese curd with the finely chopped thyme. Make a small hole in the base of each gougère and fill with the goat's curd mixture using a piping bag.

Warm the gougères in the oven at a low temperature and serve them in a basket or on a tray.

baked gruyère cheese soufflé

Serves 6

450 ml (15 fl oz) milk

55 g (2 oz) butter

55 g (2 oz) flour

4 egg yolks

160 g (5½ oz) gruyère cheese,
   grated

2 pinches of salt

2 pinches of cayenne pepper

2 tbsp chives, chopped

6 egg whites

extra grated gruyère, to serve

Preheat oven to 210°C. Warm the milk and reserve. Melt the butter in a large saucepan, add the flour and mix well for 1–2 minutes over low heat.

Remove roux from heat and gradually add the warm milk off the heat. Mix very well after each addition to ensure the mixture remains smooth.

Add the egg yolks and return to the heat. Bring to the boil and cook for 1 minute. Add the grated cheese, the seasoning and chives and mix until melted. Remove from heat and set aside.

Whip the egg whites until you have soft peaks. Fold a third of egg whites through the cheese mixture until well combined, then gently fold through the rest of the egg whites.

Butter 6 200 ml moulds or ramekins and add some mixture, not quite filling them up (they should be about three-quarters full). Bake for 20 minutes or until firm. Sprinkle with some more grated gruyère when they come out of the oven.

Serve immediately on their own, or un-mould and serve with a salad or creamy sautéed button mushrooms.

corn soup

Serves 4

8 cobs fresh corn
2 tsp olive oil
6 shallots, peeled and finely chopped
2 garlic cloves, peeled and crushed
1.5 litres (6 cups) vegetable stock
    (see recipe page 193)
500 ml (2 cups) pouring cream
salt and white pepper

Husk and clean corn, then cut kernels from cobs and discard cores.

Lightly heat olive oil in a medium-sized pan. Add shallots and garlic. Stir until transparent.

Add corn kernels and vegetable stock. Bring to the boil, then reduce heat and simmer for 40 minutes until corn is soft.

Blend soup with stick blender then add the cream and gently heat through. Adjust seasoning with salt and white pepper and serve.

fresh pea soup with mint

Serves 4

1 tbsp olive oil
6 shallots, peeled and chopped
2 garlic cloves, peeled and chopped
1 kg (2 lb) fresh garden peas,
    shelled and cooked
1.5 litres (6 cups) vegetable stock
    (see recipe page 193)
2 medium-sized desirée potatoes,
    peeled and chopped
10 mint leaves
salt and pepper
500 ml (2 cups) cream, lightly
    whipped
shredded mint leaves to garnish

Heat olive oil in a medium-sized saucepan and add shallots, garlic and half the peas. Stir until lightly cooked but do not allow to brown.

Add vegetable stock, potatoes and fresh mint. Bring to the boil, reduce heat and simmer for 40 minutes.

Blend soup with blender, then pass through fine sieve. Blend the remaining peas, sieve, and add this purée at the last minute (this creates a beautiful natural green colour).

Adjust seasoning with salt and pepper. Serve hot with cream stirred through and shredded mint leaves.

borlotti beans, tomato and cotechino sausage soup

Serves 4

250 g (8 oz) cotechino or Italian
    sausage
100 ml (3½ fl oz) olive oil
2 medium onions, peeled and
    chopped
4 garlic cloves, peeled and chopped
1 medium-sized fennel bulb, chopped
6 medium-sized very ripe soft
    tomatoes, peeled and chopped
500 g (1 lb) fresh borlotti beans,
    peeled
1 bay leaf
1.5 litres (6 cups) chicken stock
    (see recipe page 192)
2 pinches of sweet paprika
sea salt
flatleaf parsley leaves

Remove skin from sausage and crumble meat with your fingers.

Heat olive oil in saucepan, add chopped onion, garlic and fennel. Cook until golden. Add sausage meat, tomatoes, beans, bay leaf and chicken stock. Simmer for 40 minutes then add sweet paprika and sea salt.

Top with parsley before serving.

warm salad of green and yellow beans with duck confit

Serves 4

24 yellow beans

24 green beans

125 ml ($\frac{1}{2}$ cup) red wine vinegar

1 garlic clove, peeled and chopped

2 shallots, peeled and chopped

100 ml ($3\frac{1}{2}$ fl oz) walnut oil

100 ml ($3\frac{1}{2}$ fl oz) extra virgin olive oil

sea salt and milled black pepper

1 tbsp olive oil, extra

150 g (5 oz) baby spinach

100 g ($3\frac{1}{2}$ oz) pecan nuts,
    freshly roasted

4 duck legs confit, shredded
    (see recipe page 203)

Cook beans in salted boiling water until tender. Remove and cool in cold water, then halve lengthways. Reserve.

In a small saucepan, place vinegar, garlic and shallots. Heat and reduce by a quarter. Remove from heat and cool.

Once cool, add walnut oil and extra virgin olive oil while stirring. Season with sea salt and milled black pepper.

Heat extra olive oil in a pan and quickly toss washed baby spinach leaves until just wilted. Remove and place in salad bowl with green and yellow beans, duck confit, roasted pecan nuts and dressing. Toss salad and arrange on serving plates.

Note: it is always good to gently warm up your duck confit to bring out the flavours before you use it.

roast onion tart

Serves 8

1 brown onion, peeled and halved

1 Spanish onion, peeled and halved

6 spring onion bulbs, trimmed

100 ml (3½ fl oz) olive oil

1 quantity of shortcrust pastry
   (see recipe page 197)

4 eggs

150 ml (5 fl oz) crème fraîche

2 pinches of thyme leaves

1 pinch of cayenne pepper

salt

Preheat oven to 120°C. In a saucepan over medium heat, toss brown onion, Spanish onion and spring onions in olive oil until they are browned but still firm. Place on oven tray and roast slowly for 1½ hours, until well-cooked and golden brown. Remove from oven and allow to cool.

Increase oven temperature to 175°C. Line a greased 25 cm (10 in) flan dish with shortcrust pastry. Blind bake crust with beans in it for 15 minutes. Remove from oven. Arrange roasted onions on pastry in pie dish. Place on baking tray.

Lightly beat eggs with crème fraîche, thyme leaves, cayenne pepper and salt. Pour this mixture over onions and fill until just under top edge of the flan dish.

Place tart in oven and cook until egg mixture is set and pastry is cooked and golden, approximately 45 minutes. Remove from oven, allow to cool and then serve with a green salad.

duck, beetroot, goat's curd and mâche pizza

Serves 4

8 baby beetroot

1 quantity of pizza dough
   (see recipe page 196)

1 quantity of tomato pizza sauce
   (see recipe page 194)

100 g (3½ oz) grated mozzarella
   cheese, grated

100 g (3½ oz) grated parmesan
   cheese, grated

duck confit (see recipe page 203)

8 heads of mâche salad leaves

24 green beans, blanched and
   halved lengthways

1 tbsp extra virgin olive oil

400 g (13 oz) fresh goat's curd

sea salt and milled black pepper

Boil baby beetroot in salted water until they are tender and cooked. Cool and peel. Cut in quarters and leave to one side.

Preheat oven to maximum heat. Divide pizza dough into 4 and roll out pizza bases. Thinly spread pizza bases with tomato pizza sauce, then sprinkle with mozzarella and parmesan. Arrange pieces of duck confit and quartered beetroot on top. Cook in oven until base is golden and crisp.

Toss mâche with green beans and olive oil, and place on top of pizza. Finally, top with some small pieces of goat's cheese curd and sprinkle with sea salt and milled black pepper.

affettato pizza

Serves 4

1 quantity of pizza dough
(see recipe page 196)

1 quantity of tomato pizza sauce
(see recipe page 194)

100 g (3½ oz) grated parmesan
cheese, grated

100 g (3½ oz) grated mozzarella
cheese, grated

4 pinches of fresh chopped oregano
leaves

8 slices of prosciutto ham

16 slices of coppa ham

Preheat oven to maximum. Cut dough into four portions, roll out thinly and place on oven tray sprinkled with a touch of semolina.

Coat pizza bases with tomato sauce. Sprinkle with mozzarella, parmesan and chopped oregano leaves. Bake pizza in oven until golden and the base is cooked.

Remove from oven, place on a serving plate and arrange sliced meats on top. Serve uncut.

seafood risotto

Serves 4

1 litre (4 cups) good fish stock
   (see recipe page 192)

100 g (3½ oz) butter

1 large onion, diced small

2 garlic cloves, peeled and chopped

salt and pepper

400 g (13 oz) arborio, vialone nano
   or carnaroli rice

125 ml (½ cup) white wine

a knob of butter

400 g (13 oz) mixed seafood
   (including prawns, scallops,
   squid, mussels, fish pieces)

2 tbsp chlorophyll
   (see recipe page 193)

Bring the fish stock to the boil.

In another pot melt the butter and gently fry the onion until it is translucent. Add the garlic and fry till soft.

Add the rice and fry till it is nice and hot (this opens the pores of the rice). Deglaze with the white wine.

Add the hot fish stock in four batches, each time covering the rice with the liquid. Stir the rice constantly to develop the starch. At the fourth stage add the stock and remove from the heat. Season the rice at this time.

Heat a frying pan over a medium heat and add a knob of butter. While the butter is still foaming add the seafood and cook till just done.

Stir through the chlorophyll and check the seasoning. Combine the risotto and the seafood carefully so as not to break up the seafood.

Distribute between 4 warm plates and serve immediately.

rotolo pasta with broccoli, peas and ricotta

Serves 4

250 g (8 oz) rotolo pasta
1 cup broccoli florets, blanched
1 cup peas, blanched
2 tbsp soft butter
200 g (7 oz) ricotta cheese
salt

Blanch pasta in salted boiling water until almost cooked. Add broccoli and peas to the boiling water to warm up. Drain.

Add the butter and the ricotta and gently fold until your pasta is coated with the cheese. Season with a little salt.

Optional: you may also add some sliced ham and basil.

parsley and pea risotto

1 litre (4 cups) chicken or
  vegetable stock
  (see recipes pages 192–193)
1 onion, finely chopped
2 tbsp olive oil
400 g (13 oz) arborio, vialone
  nano or carnaroli rice
100 ml (3½ fl oz) white wine
  (optional)
75 g (2½ oz) cold butter
300 g (10 oz) fresh peas, blanched
100 g (3½ oz) parmesan cheese,
  grated
4 tbsp flatleaf parsley, chopped
salt and pepper

Heat the stock and allow to simmer while preparing the risotto in another pan.

Sweat onion in the olive oil until soft but not coloured. Add rice and toast for 3 minutes.

Pour in the first ladle of hot stock and stir until absorbed. Quickly add a second ladle, allowing this to be absorbed. Add half the white wine and stir until the wine is all absorbed. Add another ladle of hot stock, then the remaining wine, stirring constantly.

Continue to add stock a ladleful at a time until the rice is slightly firm but not crunchy. You may need more or less stock, depending on the rate of absorption.

When you have achieved a good texture, remove from the heat. The rice should be slightly soupy.

Add the butter to stop the heat and make the mixture creamier. Then add the blanched peas, parmesan and the parsley to finish. Adjust seasoning and serve immediately.

barramundi with parsnip and potato crust

Serves 4

2 medium parsnips, peeled

2 medium desirée potatoes, peeled

4 barramundi fillets, 180 g (6 oz)
   each

100 ml (3½ fl oz) olive oil

100 g (3½ oz) butter

2 garlic cloves, peeled and chopped

200 g (7 oz) sliced assorted
   mushrooms, e.g. shitake, Swiss
   brown and enoki

100 ml (3½ fl oz) red wine vinegar

salt and pepper

8 baby parsnips, peeled and roasted

2 bunches of English spinach,
   washed and wilted

Slice parsnips and potatoes lengthways into paper-thin ribbons. Lay a combination of these strips over each barramundi fillet.

Heat half the olive oil and butter in frying pan until foaming, then add barramundi fillets, parsnip and potato side down. Cook on low heat until parsnip and potato are golden. Turn and cook on other side.

In another frying pan, slowly heat remaining olive oil and add garlic and mushrooms. Sauté, then add vinegar and slightly reduce sauce. Remove from heat and season with salt and pepper. Finish by stirring in remaining butter.

Place mushrooms on serving plate and top with a piece of barramundi. Serve with roasted baby parsnips and wilted spinach.

braised Mediterranean fish stew

Serves 4

100 ml (3½ fl oz) olive oil

1 brown onion, sliced

2 fennel bulbs with leaves, sliced

4 garlic cloves, peeled and chopped

4 ripe tomatoes, chopped

8 yellow teardrop tomatoes, halved

200 ml (7 fl oz) white wine

8 baby carrots, peeled

2 litres (8 cups) fish stock
   (see recipe page 192)

1 bay leaf

2 pinches of saffron

salt and pepper

4 garfish fillets, deboned

4 red mullet, deboned

200 g (7 oz) white fish fillets,
   e.g. whiting

8 fresh scallops

8 green prawns, peeled

8 baby squid tubes

handful of chopped fresh herbs
   to garnish

Heat oil in a large pan, then add sliced onion and fennel and fry until soft. Add garlic and cook for 2 minutes. Add tomatoes, white wine, carrots, fish stock, bay leaf, saffron, salt and pepper. Simmer until tomatoes are soft and carrot cooked. Adjust seasoning.

Add all the seafood to the pan and simmer until fish is cooked. Garnish with herbs and serve.

garfish fillet with lemon, green vegetables and zucchini frittata

Serves 4

Zucchini Frittata

4 baby zucchini with flowers, halved
    or sliced small zucchini

1 tbsp olive oil

3 garlic cloves, peeled and chopped

2 spring onions, sliced

8 eggs

100 ml (3½ fl oz) sour cream

salt and pepper

Garfish Fillet

50 ml (1½ fl oz) olive oil

100 g (3½ oz) butter

4 garfish fillets, deboned

juice of 1 lemon

Green Vegetables

4 stalks of broccolini, blanched

100 g (3½ oz) sugar snap peas,
    blanched

100 g (3½ oz) green beans,
    blanched

handful of watercress, blanched

handful of baby spinach, blanched

50 g (1½ oz) butter

2 lemons, halved

50 ml (1½ fl oz) lemon oil

sea salt

To make zucchini frittata, preheat oven to 160°C. Grease four cups in a nonstick muffin tin.

Sauté zucchinis with olive oil, garlic and spring onions until lightly browned. Divide zucchini mixture between muffin tins.

Beat eggs with sour cream, season with salt and pepper, then pour over zucchini mixture until each of the cups is full. Bake in oven until egg has set and fritatta is golden brown on top.

To make garfish fillet, heat olive oil and butter in a frying pan, then add garfish fillets. When cooked, drizzle with lemon juice. Remove pan from heat.

To serve, cook vegetables in a saucepan with butter, then place on serving plates with garfish and lemon halves and frittata. Drizzle with lemon oil and sea salt and serve immediately.

roasted snapper with vegetable nage

Serves 4

250 ml (1 cup) fish stock
   (see recipe page 192)
3 baby carrots, peeled and sliced
2 medium pontiac potatoes, peeled
   and diced
1 fennel bulb, diced
1 leek, finely sliced
1 garlic clove, peeled and crushed
1 pinch of saffron
salt and pepper
4 snapper fillets, 180 g (6 oz) each
2 tbsp olive oil
sea salt
1 tbsp butter
12 asparagus spears, blanched

Preheat oven to 250°C.

Bring fish stock to simmer in saucepan with carrots, potatoes, fennel, leek, garlic and saffron. Adjust seasoning and cook slowly until vegetables are cooked. Remove from heat.

Brush snapper with olive oil and season with sea salt. In a hot nonstick pan heat the oil and add the butter and the seasoned snapper. Cook for 1 minute then turn over and finish in a preheated oven for another 5 minutes.

While snapper is baking, slowly heat vegetables and stock with asparagus spears.

Place snapper on serving plates and top with 3 asparagus spears each. Spoon vegetables and stock over the snapper and serve immediately.

ocean trout ballotine with parsnip brandade

Serves 8

Parsnip Brandade

4 medium desiree potatoes

4 garlic cloves, peeled

150 ml (5 fl oz) cream

200 g (7 oz) salt cod, soaked
   overnight in cold water

2 parsnips, roasted and puréed

salt and pepper

Ocean Trout Ballotine

200 g (7 oz) baby spinach

200 g (7 oz) rocket

3 cloves of roasted garlic

100 g (3½ oz) unsalted butter

salt and pepper

2 sides of ocean trout
   (medium-size), pin bones and
   grey fat removed

To make parsnip brandade, bring the potato and the garlic cloves to the boil, starting in cold water. Cook until potato is done. Strain. Mash the potatoes with the garlic, using the hot cream to adjust the consistency.

Add the soaked cod (cleaned and shredded) and the parsnip purée. Adjust the seasoning.

To make ocean trout ballotine, blanch spinach and rocket and refresh in iced water then squeeze dry. Chop coarsely with the roasted garlic and mix with the soft butter. Season well with salt and pepper.

Set the ocean trout on a board (inside flesh down) and place half the spinach and rocket mixture in the centre of the fillet. Repeat with remaining ingredients. Fold over to create a ballotine (large sausage shape). Wrap in plastic wrap and poach in tepid water for 15 minutes. Remove plastic wrap.

To serve, slice each ballotine immediately into 4 portions. Set on the brandade and sprinkle with sea salt.

salmon carpaccio
with squid ink noodles

Serves 4

Salmon Carpaccio

250 g (8 oz) salmon steak,
   skin removed

a little olive oil

Squid Ink Noodles

½ fennel bulb, diced small

1 stick of celery, diced small

juice of 1 lemon

3 tbsp extra virgin olive oil

salt and pepper

160 g (5 oz) fresh squid ink
   noodles, blanched

1 quantity of pickled cucumbers
   (see recipe page 202)

fennel tips and celery leaves,
   to garnish

To make salmon carpaccio, trim the salmon of any darker, oily parts and cut widthways into 4 pieces.

Slice each piece of salmon from the top, nearly in two, like a butterfly.

Place a sheet of plastic wrap on a heavy cutting board, brush with a touch of olive oil.

Place salmon on board, brush with a little oil, cover with another sheet of plastic wrap and, using a wooden mallet or heavy pan, gently pound each piece of salmon until you have a large circular piece. Put the salmon aside on a plate. Repeat with the remainder of the salmon pieces.

To make squid ink noodles, marinate the noodles, diced fennel and celery in the lemon juice and olive oil. Season with salt and pepper. Allow to marinate for 10–15 minutes. Reserve.

To serve, lay the salmon on a serving plate. Mix the blanched noodles with the pickled cucmbers. Place a small amount on top of the salmon.

Garnish with the fennel tips, baby celery leaves, cracked pepper and salt.

Drizzle with the leftover marinade from the noodles.

roast salmon with black olive crust and spinach purée

Serves 4

2 garlic cloves, peeled and chopped

4 shallots, peeled and chopped

50 ml (1½ fl oz) olive oil

100 g (3½ oz) Kalamata olives, deseeded and chopped

small handful of chopped flatleaf parsley

4 salmon fillets, 180 g (6 oz) each

200 ml (7 fl oz) fish stock

50 g (1½ oz) butter

4 desiree potatoes, peeled and sliced

salt and pepper

200 g (7 oz) fresh spinach purée (see recipe page 199)

Sauté garlic and shallots in pan with olive oil until golden. Remove from stove and allow to cool. Add olives and parsley and mix. Press this mixture onto top of salmon fillets.

Place fish stock, butter, sliced potatoes and salt and pepper in saucepan and simmer over low heat until potatoes are cooked. Remove from heat.

Preheat oven to 180°C. Place salmon fillets on lightly oiled baking paper on a baking tray. Roast in oven until fish is cooked, approximately 6 minutes.

Warm through spinach purée. Place potatoes on serving plates with warm spinach purée, top with a roasted salmon fillet and serve.

baked jewfish with squid and herb crust and tomato sauce

Serves 4

Sauce

100 ml (3½ fl oz) olive oil

1 brown onion, peeled and chopped

4 garlic cloves, peeled and chopped

150 ml (5 fl oz) white wine

1 tbsp tomato paste

12 medium-sized ripe tomatoes, chopped

salt and pepper

4 squid tubes

150 g (5 oz) fresh breadcrumbs

handful of fresh chopped herbs, such as parsley, fennel, thyme, spinach

4 jewfish cutlets, centre bone removed

To make sauce, heat half the olive oil in saucepan until hot. Add chopped onion and garlic and cook until golden. Add white wine and reduce by half. Add tomato paste and chopped tomatoes and simmer for 1 hour over low heat. Season with salt and pepper.

To make jewfish, preheat oven to 180°C. Slice squid finely then mix with breadcrumbs, herbs and remaining olive oil. Press mixture on top of each cutlet.

In a baking dish, spread sauce over the bottom and place cutlets on top. Cook for approximately 20 minutes, or until crumbs are golden and fish is cooked.

To serve, place tomato sauce on serving plate and top with a cutlet. Serve immediately.

chicken with mushroom stuffing

Serves 4

1.2 kg organic chicken

50 g (1½ oz) dried porcini
   mushrooms

1 cup Swiss brown mushrooms

2 field mushrooms

12 sage leaves

handful of flatleaf parsley

1 knob butter

12 shallots, peeled and chopped

4 garlic cloves, peeled and chopped

1 tbsp olive oil

2 large handfuls of fresh white
   breadcrumbs

200 g (7 oz) soft butter

salt and pepper

8 baby leeks

400 g (13 oz) small potatoes

1 tbsp softened butter

100 ml (3½ fl oz) chicken stock
   (see recipe page 192)

Preheat oven to 200°C.

Wash chicken and dry with paper towel, then run your fingers under the skin to create a pocket that can be stuffed, starting from the breast and wing end. Set aside in refrigerator.

Soak porcini mushrooms in warm water until soft. Remove and chop into small dice. Chop Swiss brown and field mushrooms with sage and parsley.

Heat knob of butter in frying pan and brown shallots and garlic. Add all the chopped mushrooms and 1 tablespoon olive oil and fry until cooked.

In a mixing bowl, combine breadcrumbs, mushrooms, sage, parsley, shallots and garlic and mix with softened butter. Season with salt and pepper. Insert some mushroom stuffing under the skin of the chicken and the remainder inside the chicken.

Place chicken, baby leeks and potatoes in a baking dish. Brush with butter and season with salt and pepper. Roast in oven until chicken starts to brown, then reduce heat to 165°C and cook for another hour or until chicken is cooked.

Remove from oven and place chicken, leeks and potatoes on serving plate.

Reheat pan juices and stir in chicken stock. Reduce until it is a sauce consistency. Pour over chicken and serve.

braised spiced chicken with lentils and roasted vegetables

Serves 4

2 medium carrots

2 medium parsnips

2 small leeks

4 chicken thighs, thigh bone in
    and skin on

1 tbsp smoked paprika

2 tsp five-spice powder

150 ml (5 fl oz) olive oil

200 g (7 oz) baby lentils, soaked

4 garlic cloves, peeled and chopped

1 litre (4 cups) reduced chicken
    stock (see recipe page 192)

salt and pepper

50 g (1½ oz) flatleaf parsley,
    roughly chopped

Preheat oven to 180°C.

Peel carrots and parsnips and cut in quarters lengthways. Wash and clean leeks then cut lengthways into halves.

Tie chicken thighs crosswise with twine. Sprinkle with paprika and five-spice powder.

Heat olive oil in a braising pan and brown the chicken, carrots, parsnips and leeks, then add lentils, garlic and chicken stock and season with salt and pepper.

Place pan into oven and cook for 30 minutes. Remove chicken and vegetables and keep warm.

Strain the braising stock into a clean pot and boil down until you have a good-looking sauce. Add the parsley and if the sauce is too liquid, thicken with 1 tablespoon of cornflour diluted in a bit of cold water.

Pour over the chicken and vegetables and then serve.

pork rillettes

Serves 6

300 g (10 oz) rock salt

3 cinnamon quills, crushed

5 cloves

2 star anise

3 garlic cloves, peeled

2 shallots, peeled

8 white peppercorns, crushed

1 bunch of lemon thyme

1 kg (2 lb) pork belly bones with
skin removed

3 litres of rendered pork back fat
(ask your butcher or use olive
oil instead)

white pepper

To make the marinade, mix together the salt, cinnamon, cloves, star anise, garlic, shallots, white peppercorns and lemon thyme, saving 4 stems of the thyme for later.

Rub the marinade ingredients liberally over the pork belly and leave to marinate in the fridge overnight. Wash marinade off the pork belly and pat dry.

Preheat oven to 120°C. Heat the rendered pork fat in a deep roasting pan on the stove to blood temperature, and submerge the pork belly into it. Cover with a lid or foil and place into the oven. Cook gently until the flesh can be pulled apart easily, 2–3 hours.

When cooked, cool pork in the fat until it is at a temperature that allows you to handle it without burning yourself. Drain the fat off the pork belly and gently pull the pork belly apart into thin strips.

Once it is all shredded, add a little of the pork fat, just enough to bind the meat together. Season with milled white pepper and the leaves from the reserved lemon thyme.

Serve with toasted brioche or sourdough with cornichons.

duck confit with smoked pork flank, lentils and savoy cabbage

Serves 4

1 small savoy cabbage

8 finger leeks

100 ml (3½ fl oz) olive oil

2 garlic cloves, peeled and crushed

2 ripe tomatoes, peeled and roughly
   chopped

handful of flatleaf parsley

several sprigs of sage

salt and pepper

4 thick slices of smoked pork flank

200 g (7 oz) dry lentils, soaked for
   20 minutes

1 litre (4 cups) strong chicken stock
   (see recipe page 192)

4 confit duck legs
   (see recipe page 203)

Preheat oven to 140°C. Blanch savoy cabbage in boiling water and remove the outer leaves and pat dry. Reserve outer leaves and chop remaining cabbage into strips. Wash and clean leeks.

Heat olive oil in ovenproof dish and add garlic and leeks. Brown lightly. Add tomatoes and cabbage strips, parsley and sage and cook until the cabbage is wilted (this will take around 10 minutes). Season with salt and pepper. Remove from stove and allow to cool.

Take a whole cabbage leaf and place 2 leeks, one quarter of the cabbage mixture and 1 slice of pork flank inside. Roll up, folding sides in. Repeat to make 4 cabbage rolls.

Heat a little olive oil in braising pan and brown cabbage rolls lightly. Add lentils and the chicken stock. Place in oven and allow to braise for 30 minutes, until sauce is reduced.

Take confit duck legs and place into sauce around cabbage rolls and allow 15 minutes extra cooking.

Place cabbage rolls and duck legs on serving plate and pour lentil and chicken jus over top, then serve.

double lamb cutlet with mushrooms wrapped in puff pastry

Serves 4

200 g (7oz) Swiss brown
   mushrooms
100 g (3½ oz) dried porcini
   mushrooms, soaked and drained
200 g (7 oz) field mushrooms
100 ml (3½ fl oz) olive oil
4 garlic cloves, peeled and chopped
8 shallots, peeled and chopped
6 rosemary leaves
2 sprigs of thyme leaves
salt and pepper
2 tbsp olive oil, extra
4 double lamb cutlets, trimmed
salt and pepper
2 sheets of puff pastry,
   30 cm x 30 cm
egg wash
blanced baby green beans to serve
lamb jus (optional)

Clean mushrooms and chop finely. Heat olive oil in frying pan then add garlic and shallots and brown. Add chopped mushrooms along with rosemary and thyme. Sauté slowly over low heat until dry. Remove from heat and season with salt and pepper and allow to cool.

Heat extra olive oil in a frying pan. Quickly sauté lamb on both sides to seal the meat then remove from pan and cool. Season with salt and pepper then press mushroom mixture on top.

Take a long strip of puff pastry and wrap around cutlet to meet at bottom. Place on oiled baking try and allow to rest in the refrigerator for 30 minutes. Brush pastry with egg wash.

Preheat oven to 200°C. Place lamb into oven and cook for 15 minutes, or until pastry has risen and is golden brown. Remove and place on serving plates with baby green beans and lamb jus, then serve.

veal shank 'pot au feu'

Serves 4

16 baby carrots
4 baby turnips
8 shallots
8 small kipfler potatoes
200 g (7 oz) fresh borlotti beans
4 vine-ripened tomatoes
4 veal shanks, French trimmed
handful each of parsley, thyme,
    oregano
salt and milled black pepper

Peel carrots, turnips, shallots and leave whole. Wash kipfler potatoes and pod fresh borlotti beans. Blanch and peel tomatoes.

Place veal shanks in a pot with enough cold water to cover, then place on stove and bring to simmer for 10 minutes. Remove from heat. Pour off water and rinse veal. Refill with fresh cold water to cover veal and add all other ingredients. Season with salt and pepper. Return to heat and allow to simmer very slowly. After 30 minutes remove the vegetables and set aside. Continue cooking the veal for another hour.

Remove veal and place on serving plates with the reheated vegetables in the stock. Pour over cooking liquid and serve.

pepper steak with French-style peas and potato gratin

Serves 4

Pepper Steak

12 beef mignonettes, 70 g (2½ oz)
   each from the beef tenderloin
80 g (3 oz) freshly milled black
   pepper
50 ml (1½ fl oz) olive oil
2 garlic cloves, peeled and crushed
8 thin slices of speck or bacon
250 g (8 oz) freshly podded green
   peas, blanched
1 whole butter lettuce, cut into
   thin strips
100 g (3½ oz) butter
salt

1 quantity of potato gratin
   (see recipe page 198)

To make pepper steak, sprinkle both sides of each fillet steak with milled pepper. Heat frying pan with olive oil then sauté fillet steaks until cooked as desired. Place on serving plates.

In the same pan add crushed garlic, finely sliced speck or bacon and cook until brown. Add blanched peas and lettuce to warm through.

Remove the pan from heat then add butter. Stir until butter is melted then add sliced lettuce and season with salt. Spoon this mixture over steaks and serve with potato gratin.

crisp meringue with mango passionfruit custard

Serves 6

Meringue

3 egg whites

260 g (8 $\frac{1}{2}$ oz) sugar

2 drops of vanilla essence

$\frac{1}{2}$ tsp vinegar

1 tbsp cornflour

1 tbsp icing sugar

1 quantity of passionfruit custard
   (see recipe page 204)

200 ml (7 fl oz) cream, whipped

2 mangoes, peeled and diced

mint leaves to garnish

To make meringue, preheat oven to 120°C.

Whisk together the egg whites, sugar, vanilla and vinegar for 10 minutes. Add the sifted cornflour and icing sugar and whisk in.

Pipe or spoon meringues into 6 tall egg rings or directly onto a tray lined with silicon paper and bake for 45 minutes. Turn the tray around in the oven to ensure the meringue bakes evenly and bake for a further 20 minutes.

To serve, combine custard with equal amounts of softly whipped fresh cream. Spread on top of meringue and serve with freshly diced mango. Garnish with mint leaves if desired.

warm rhubarb and strawberry pies

Serves 6

Pastry

300 g (10 oz) cold unsalted butter

500 g (1 lb) plain flour

1 tsp salt

1 tbsp castor sugar

3 eggs

Rhubarb and Strawberry Filling

500 g (1 lb) rhubarb

200 g (7 oz) castor sugar

400 g (13 oz) strawberries, halved

1 tbsp cornflour

2 drops vanilla essence

Topping

1 bunch of fresh rhubarb

400 ml (13 fl oz) water

500 g (16 oz) castor sugar

$\frac{1}{2}$ vanilla bean, split open lengthways

egg wash

To make pastry, rub the cold unsalted butter into the sifted flour, with the salt and castor sugar. Add the eggs one at a time. Mix until combined. Refrigerate for a couple of hours.

To make filling, do not peel the rhubarb. Cut into pieces 2 cm long. Cook the rhubarb with sugar in a heavy-based pan over medium heat until mixture is thick and all the liquid has evaporated, about half an hour.

Sprinkle the cornflour over the strawberries and toss. Add the strawberries to the cooked rhubarb, bring back to the boil and cook for another 2 minutes. Pour the mixture into a shallow bowl, stir in the vanilla essence and allow to cool. Refrigerate.

To make topping, preheat oven to 160°C. Scrape the rhubarb stalks, removing any fibrous threads, and cut into 4 cm lengths. Arrange them in a baking dish.

Put water, sugar and vanilla bean into a pan and stir until the sugar has dissolved. Boil the syrup, without stirring, for 3 minutes over gentle heat. Remove from the heat. Pour the hot liquid over the prepared rhubarb. Cover the dish with a lid or foil and bake for 25 minutes or until the rhubarb is tender. Allow to cool.

To assemble pies, preheat oven to 185°C. Roll the dough out to 2 mm thick. Spray 6 pie moulds, 9 cm diameter and 2 cm deep, with nonstick spray. Line base of pie moulds with pastry and cut pastry tops to fit.

Fill the tarts with the cooled filling. Brush the edges with egg wash and place the pastry tops on. Press the edges together to seal and then trim excess pastry. Cut the edges. Cut a hole in the middle of the tarts.

Brush egg wash over the tops and sprinkle with castor sugar. Bake the tarts for 10 minutes.

To serve, cool down the pies slightly so that they are warm rather than hot. Serve with some of the rhubarb topping and vanilla icecream at the last minute.

passionfruit panna cotta with tropical ratatouille

Serves 8

Passionfruit Panna Cotta
100 ml (3½ fl oz) milk
240 ml (8 fl oz) cream
120 g (4 oz) sugar
2 leaves of gelatine, softened
140 ml (4½ fl oz) passionfruit
   pulp, seeds removed

Tropical Ratatouille
1 mango
½ papaya
1 kiwifruit
½ rockmelon
10 strawberries

To make passionfruit panna cotta, bring the milk, cream and sugar to the boil. Add the gelatine and strain. Cool over ice until the mixture starts to thicken.

Add the passionfruit pulp and pour into 8 lightly greased one-cup plastic dariole moulds. Refrigerate until set.

To make tropical ratatouille, dice all the fruit into small cubes.

To serve, unmould the panna cotta and serve with the tropical ratatouille

stonefruit parfait

Serves 4

Roasted Vanilla Peaches
4 peaches or other stonefruit
80 g (3 oz) sugar
1 vanilla bean

Parfait
100 g (3^1/$_2$ oz) sugar
3 egg yolks
1 vanilla bean, scraped
100 g (3^1/$_2$ oz) diced blanched
   peaches (see recipe)
300 ml (10 fl oz) soft whipped
   cream

Nougatine Biscuit
100 g (3^1/$_2$ oz) sugar
100 ml (3^1/$_2$ fl oz) liquid glucose
50 g (1^1/$_2$ oz) butter
100 g (3^1/$_2$ oz) crushed flaked
   almonds

To make roasted vanilla peaches, preheat oven to 200°C.

Halve the peaches and destone them. Plunge into boiling water for 10–15 seconds and then into iced water. This should enable the skin to peel off easily. Dice two of the peaches for the parfait and reserve the others for roasting.

Place the halved peaches on a baking tray, sprinkle with sugar and place vanilla bean in the centre. Bake for 10 minutes, set aside to cool and then dice them.

To make the parfait, whisk sugar, egg yolks and vanilla in a bowl over a pan of barely simmering water until the sugar has dissolved. Remove from the heat and whip until cool and foamy.

Fold in the diced peaches and the cream. Pour into a 1.1 litre mould and freeze. (At Bathers' we use a triangular mould.)

To make the nougatine biscuit, preheat the oven to 180°C.

Boil the sugar and glucose to a light caramel. Remove from heat and whisk in the butter until it emulsifies. Fold in the almonds until they caramelise slightly. Pour mixture onto baking parchment. Place another sheet of parchment on top and roll firmly to 3 mm thick. Take off the top sheet and place the nougatine in the oven until it softens but does not spread.

Remove from the oven and cut to desired shape while still hot.

To serve, place a nougatine biscuit on the serving plate. Remove the parfait from the mould and, using a knife dipped in hot water, cut a slice of parfait slightly smaller than the nougatine biscuit and immediately set it on the nougatine. Top with another piece of nougatine and serve with the roasted vanilla peaches.

almond tart with grilled nectarines

Serves 8

Almond Filling

200 g (7 oz) butter

160 g (5½ oz) sugar

6 egg yolks

200 g (7 oz) ground almonds

pinch of salt

dash of vanilla essence

2 tbsp apricot or other jam

Tart Case

1 quantity of sweet pastry
(see recipe page 197)

Grilled Nectarines

8 nectarines

2 tbsp brown sugar

1 tbsp chopped mint

Cream

300 ml (10 fl oz) softly whipped
cream

75 g (2½ oz) icing sugar

dash of vanilla essence

100 ml (3½ fl oz) crème fraîche

2 tsp lemon juice

icing sugar

To make almond filling, cream the butter and the sugar.

Add the egg yolks slowly. Finally, add the almonds, salt and vanilla extract and mix until all the ingredients are incorporated.

To make tart, preheat oven to 180°C. Line a greased fluted 25 cm dish with pastry and trim edges. Spread the jam in the base and top with almond filling. Bake for 30 minutes or until golden brown.

To make the grilled nectarines, cut the cheek of the nectarine and place in a baking tray, skin side down. Sprinkle with brown sugar. Bake until soft and top with chopped mint.

To make cream, whisk together the cream, sugar and vanilla. Fold in the crème fraîche and lemon juice.

To serve, cut tart into 8 pieces. Place tart piece on a serving plate with the nectarine cheeks. Dust tart with icing sugar and serve with cream.

baked apple puddings with maple syrup sauce

Serves 6

Baked Apple Puddings

285 g (9 oz) brown sugar

2 eggs

125 g (4 oz) butter, melted

345 g (11 oz) self-raising flour

1 tsp ground cinnamon

220 ml (7½ fl oz) milk

100 g (3½ oz) raisins

240 g (8 oz) apples, peeled and diced

Maple Syrup Sauce

170 g (6 oz) brown sugar

170 ml (6 fl oz) maple syrup

300 ml (10 fl oz) water

1 apple, peeled and finely diced

2 tbsp cornflour

225 g (7½ oz) diced butter

To make baked apple puddings, preheat oven to 165°C.

Mix together the brown sugar and eggs until smooth. Add the butter, then the sifted flour and cinnamon. Add the milk and mix in the raisins and the apple.

Pour into greased moulds (the size of a small cup) and bake for 15–20 minutes until cooked and golden brown.

To make maple syrup sauce, boil brown sugar, maple syrup and water together. Add the diced apple. Dilute the cornflour in a little bit of cold water, then add to the syrup mixture. Bring back to the boil.

Take sauce off the heat and whisk in the butter until fully melted. This sauce will keep at room temperature for a day. Just warm it up when you need it.

banana tatins with caramel sauce and coconut icecream

Serves 6

Banana Tatins

250 g (8 oz) sugar

water (enough to make the sugar wet)

75 g (2½ oz) butter

6 ripe bananas

6 puff pastry discs

1 quantity of caramel sauce (see recipe page 204)

1 quantity of coconut icecream (see recipe page 205)

To make banana tatins, preheat oven to 200°C. Caramelise the sugar and water to a deep golden caramel. Whisk in the butter until totally combined. Pour the mixture into the moulds (10 cm in diameter) until it's 5 cm deep.

Slice the ripe bananas 2 cm thick and fill the moulds tightly. Cover with the puff pastry discs (rolled 3 mm thick and cut to size).

Bake in the oven until the pastry is golden brown and the caramel is bubbling.

To serve, carefully turn the tatins onto the serving plates.

Pour some warm caramel sauce around the edge of the tatins. Scoop some coconut icecream onto the centre of the tatins.

mascarpone and grape flan with poached figs and pistachio crunch

Serves 6

Poached Figs

500 ml (2 cups) water

500 g (1 lb) sugar

1 vanilla pod

1 tbsp orange blossom water

6 ripe figs

Mascarpone

100 ml (3$\frac{1}{2}$ fl oz) cream

juice of one lemon juice

300 g (10 oz) mascarpone

Grape Syrup

400 ml (13 fl oz) grape juice

100 g (3$\frac{1}{2}$ oz) sugar

500 g (1 lb) seedless grapes

pistachio crunch

   (see recipe page 205)

To poach figs, boil the water, sugar, vanilla and orange blossom until sugar has dissolved. Pour over the figs and allow to cool.

To make mascarpone, bring the mascarpone to room temperature by leaving it on the kitchen bench for 15 minutes. Whip the cream to a soft consistency and then mix it with the lemon juice and the mascarpone.

To make grape syrup, combine grape juice and sugar in a heavy-based pan and reduce by half over medium heat.

To assemble, cut the grapes in 2 and mix with the mascarpone mixture. Grease some large egg rings and fill to the rim with the mascarpone and grape mixture. Chill for 1 hour.

To serve, run a hot knife around the inside of the egg ring and turn out onto the serving plate. Sprinkle pistachio crunch over the top, drizzle with some grape syrup and serve with a poached fig.

chocolate délice

Serves 6

Almond Sponge

70 g (2½ oz) sugar

2 egg whites

15 g (½ oz) plain flour, sifted

50 g (1½ oz) ground almonds

Chocolate Mousse Filling

1 tbsp water

3 tsp glucose or golden syrup

1 gelatine leaf, soaked until soft

75 g (2½ oz) dark chocolate, chopped

150 ml (5 fl oz) cream, whipped

Chocolate Glaze

150 ml (5 fl oz) water

50 ml (1½ fl oz) cream

120 g (4 oz) sugar

50 g (1½ oz) cocoa powder, sifted

155 ml (5 fl oz) cream

215 g (7½ oz) dark chocolate

To make almond sponge, preheat oven to 230°C.

Whisk the sugar and egg whites until stiff peaks form.

Fold in the dry ingredients and spread about a 5 mm thickness onto a greaseproof paper-lined baking tray.

Bake for 4–5 minutes until lightly golden brown. Allow to cool and using a 7.5 cm diameter cake ring as a guide, cut out 6 sponge circles.

To make chocolate mousse filling, boil the water and glucose. Add the gelatine and when melted pour the liquid over the chocolate and stir until smooth.

Cool for a few minutes and fold in the softly whipped cream. Pour into the cake rings lined with the almond sponge bases. Level off with a palette knife and chill overnight in the fridge.

To make chocolate glaze, boil half the water with the smaller quantity of cream. Take the rest of the water and mix to a paste with the sugar and cocoa powder. Add this paste to the boiling water and cream and reboil. Pass through a sieve and allow to cool to room temperature.

Bring the larger quantity of cream to the boil and pour over the chocolate. Stir until smooth. Mix with the rest of the ingredients.

To assemble, remove the cake from the ring by using a hot knife. Place on a cooling wire over a tray.

Pour over the room temperature glaze (if it is a bit thick warm very slightly). Chill in the fridge until ready to serve.

chocolate tart

Serves 12

Tart Base
120 g (4 oz) butter
115 g (4 oz) sugar
a pinch of salt
dash of vanilla essence
50 g (1½ oz) cocoa powder
120 g (4 oz) plain flour

Ganache Filling
400 ml (13 fl oz) cream
525 g (17 oz) chocolate

To make tart base, preheat oven to 180°C.

Cream butter and sugar. Add the rest of the ingredients and mix to a dough. Roll to 3 mm thick and line a greased tart ring 23.5 cm in diameter and 3 cm deep.

Bake blind for 8–10 minutes. Allow to cool and fill to the top with the ganache filling.

To make ganache filling, bring the cream to the boil, pour over the chocolate and whisk until smooth.

To serve, slice the tart into 12 pieces and serve with vanilla icecream and whipped cream.

pots of chocolate

Serves 6

150 ml (5 fl oz) milk

450 ml (15 fl oz) cream

9 egg yolks

90 g (3 oz) sugar

150 g (5 oz) dark chocolate

Preheat oven to 100°C.

Bring the milk and cream to a boil. Mix the egg yolks and sugar together with a whisk. Pour on some of the boiling liquid, whisk, and add to the rest of the liquid.

Remove from the heat and stir in the chocolate until it melts.

Pour into 6 50 ml ramekins and stand in a baking dish. Fill with enough hot water to come halfway up the sides. Bake for 30–40 minutes until set.

BASICS

chicken stock

1.5 kg (3 lb) chicken bones

2 litres (8 cups) water

1 medium carrot, peeled and chopped

1 stalk celery, chopped

1 small leek, chopped and washed

1 medium onion, peeled and chopped

1 bay leaf

handful of fresh sage

handful of flatleaf parsley

Place chicken bones in cold water. Bring to boil for 5 minutes, then strain, discarding water.

Wash bones then return bones to pot with 2 litres (8 cups) fresh water and all other ingredients.

Simmer slowly for 4 hours without any bubbling.

Strain, cool, then store in refrigerator for up to 3 days or freeze in an airtight container.

fish stock

head and bones of 2 snapper or
  other white fish

1 medium onion, peeled and chopped

1 medium carrot, peeled and chopped

1 small leek, chopped and washed

1 stalk celery, chopped

2 litres (8 cups) water

1 bay leaf

handful of flatleaf parsley

150 ml (5 fl oz) white wine

Place all ingredients in stockpot, bring to the boil and then simmer for 20 minutes.

Strain through damp muslin cloth that is sitting in a colander over a large bowl.

Allow stock to cool, then keep in refrigerator for 2 days or freeze.

vegetable stock

¼ small white cabbage

2 carrots, peeled

2 leeks, washed

1 large white onion

¼ bunch of celery

2 litres (8 cups) water

handful of flatleaf parsley

2 sprigs of thyme

6 garlic cloves, peeled and crushed

sea salt

Chop all vegetables into small pieces. Place into medium-sized saucepan, then add water, herbs and a little salt. Bring to boil and simmer for 30 minutes.

Cool without straining and store in refrigerator until needed. Strain before use. Store in the fridge for up to 5 days.

chlorophyll

2 bunches of English spinach, washed and patted dry

Put English spinach through a juicer and then pass through a fine sieve. Place in a pan on the stove and cook over a low heat until tepid, making sure you do not overheat.

Remove immediately from the stove and pour the liquid into a sieve double-lined with wet cheesecloth. Place the sieve over a bowl and leave in the fridge overnight to drain the excess water.

Scrape off the chlorophyll—this should give you about 1 tablespoon—and store in a covered bowl.

hollandaise sauce

100 ml (3½ fl oz) white wine vinegar

2 shallots, peeled and finely chopped

1 sprig of tarragon

1 pinch of white pepper

6 egg yolks

1 litre (4 cups) clarified butter,
    lukewarm

salt and pepper

1 lemon

Boil white wine vinegar with shallots, tarragon and pepper until reduced by half. Remove from stove, strain and cool.

Place egg yolks and reduction in the top of a double boiler on low heat and whisk until ribbons begin to form and the egg mixture is quite white and getting thicker.

Remove from heat and continue to whisk, very slowly adding the clarified butter. If the sauce becomes too thick, add a small drop of hot water to thin the mixture.

When all the butter has been added, season with salt and pepper. Squeeze the juice of the lemon into the sauce, whisk to combine and place in a warm spot until ready to serve.

tomato pizza sauce

1 kg (2 lb) very red, soft, very ripe
    tomatoes, skin removed

150 ml (5 fl oz) olive oil

1 medium onion, chopped

6 shallots, peeled and chopped

6 garlic cloves, peeled and crushed

1 bay leaf

250 g (8 oz) tomato paste

small handful each of chopped
    flatleaf parsley, oregano and sage

salt and black pepper

Chop tomatoes roughly. Heat oil in medium-sized saucepan, then add onion and shallots and cook until lightly golden. Add garlic and bay leaf and cook for another minute.

Add chopped tomatoes and blend lightly with a stick blender. Add tomato paste and herbs, then simmer on low heat for 20 minutes. Finish with salt and milled black pepper.

Cool and refrigerate for 3–4 days until needed.

chunky tomato sauce

1 kg (2 lb) very ripe roma tomatoes,
    cored
liberal quantity of extra virgin olive oil
1 large onion, diced
2 garlic cloves, peeled and chopped
salt and pepper
1 cup of basil leaves

Preheat oven to 250°C.

Cut the tomatoes in half, squeeze to remove excess seeds and toss in some of the oil. Roast the tomatoes in the oven until the skins blister. Discard the skins and chop tomatoes roughly.

In a medium-sized pan heat some more of the oil and cook the onion and garlic until soft.

Add the tomatoes and cook for 15–20 minutes.

Season the sauce and stir in the basil leaves. Add some extra virgin olive oil and cool the sauce. Store in the fridge for up to 3–4 days.

romesco sauce

8 medium dried oncho chillies
2 small fresh chillies
4 tomatoes, roasted and peeled
4 capsicums, roasted and peeled
125 g (4 oz) almonds, blanched
    and peeled
125 g (4 oz) hazelnuts, blanched
    and peeled
1 cinnamon quill
1 tbsp olive oil
red wine vinegar
salt and pepper
4 slices of bread, no crusts, and fried

Soak the oncho chillies in warm water for two hours.

Chop the chillies, tomatoes, capsicums, nuts and, with the cinnamon quill, fry in oil for about 10 minutes. Season with vinegar, salt and pepper and discard the cinnamon quill.

Add the crumbled fried bread and pound in a mortar or pulse in a blender until the paste is smooth.

chilli relish

100 ml (3 $\frac{1}{2}$ fl oz) olive oil

3 shallots, peeled and sliced

4 garlic cloves, peeled and chopped

2 pinches of paprika powder

4 large dried red chillies, deseeded and
    finely chopped

4 large fresh red chillies, finely sliced

juice of 1 lemon

In a medium-sized frying pan add olive oil, shallots, garlic and paprika powder. Cook slowly until ingredients are soft.

Add both chillies then cook until chillies are soft. Remove from heat then add lemon juice. Cool and store for up to 1 week in the fridge.

pizza dough

300 g (10 oz) plain flour

12 g ($\frac{1}{2}$ oz) fresh yeast or 6 g ($\frac{1}{4}$ oz)
    dry yeast

1 tbsp of salt

30 ml (1 fl oz) olive oil

150 ml (5 fl oz) cold water

Mix flour, yeast, salt, olive oil and water together. Knead by hand or in a bread machine until dough is smooth and elastic, about 5–10 minutes.

Place dough in a bowl and cover with a cloth. Allow to prove in a warm place until doubled in volume (about 45 minutes). Knock back dough.

shortcrust pastry

1 kg (2 lb) plain flour

30 g (1 oz) salt

500 g (1 lb) cold butter, cubed into
    small pieces

1 egg, lightly beaten

300 ml (10 fl oz) cold still mineral water

Sift the flour and salt together. Add the cold butter and rub with your hands until you have a light crumb consistency.

Add the whisked egg and the cold water in one go. Fold gently without overworking. Dust the dough with a touch of flour and rest in the fridge for 2 hours.

sweet pastry

200 g (7 oz) butter

200 g (7 oz) sugar

2 eggs

dash of vanilla extract

400 g (13 oz) plain flour

pinch of salt

Cream together the butter and the sugar. Slowly add the eggs and vanilla. Add the sifted flour and salt and mix to a dough.

Refrigerate for 2 hours.

potato gratin

4 large potatoes

500 ml (2 cups) milk

2 garlic cloves, peeled and crushed

100 ml ($3^1/_2$ fl oz) cream

salt

100 g ($3^1/_2$ oz) grated parmesan
  cheese

Preheat oven to 160°C.

Peel the potatoes and trim the ends off. Slice each potato into 6 equally thick slices and cut round with a cutter if desired.

In a saucepan add the milk and potatoes and simmer for 2 minutes. Drain the potatoes and discard the milk.

Layer the potatoes (one per person) in 4 buttered individual gratin dishes. Bring the cream to the boil with the garlic and salt to taste. Strain the cream. Pour the cream over the potatoes to fill the ramekins to the top of the potato. Sprinkle with parmesan cheese and place gratin dishes on a baking tray.

Cook in oven until golden on top and potatoes are cooked when tested with a skewer.

potato purée

500 g (1 lb) desiree potatoes (or any
  other good mashing variety)

100 g ($3^1/_2$ oz) cold butter, diced

salt and pepper

100 ml ($3^1/_2$ fl oz) cream or milk,
  warmed

Drop potatoes into cold salted water, bring to the boil and cook until soft. If you are using new potatoes, cook them with the skin on to avoid an elastic texture, otherwise, peel the potatoes before cooking.

Purée them through a rice presser or use a hand masher. Do not use a blender or food processor as this will ruin the texture.

Add cold butter, mix, then adjust the seasoning.

Just before serving, gradually add the cream or milk until you achieve the right consistency.

There is no standard recipe for the perfect purée, everything depends on the quality and variety of potato you use and on the time of the year.

spinach purée

1 garlic clove, peeled and finely chopped

2 shallots, peeled and finely chopped

50 g (1^1/$_2$ oz) butter

2 bunches of English spinach, leaves
    picked off the stems

salt and pepper

To make spinach purée, sweat off the garlic and the shallots in half the butter, add the spinach and sweat off until cooked.

Drain really well and place in a food processor. Blend into a fine purée while adding the rest of the butter. Season and set aside.

creamed corn

The canned product is good but the homemade version is well worth making.

3 cobs of corn

water to cover

1 tsp sugar

pinch of salt

1 tbsp butter

Remove the kernels from the cobs of corn. Cover the corn with water and add the sugar and salt.

Cover the corn with greaseproof paper and cook for 20 minutes or until corn is cooked.

Purée in a food processor and stir in the butter.

preserved lemon

10 lemons

1 box of sea salt flakes

10 cinnamon quills

10 cloves

100 g (3½ oz) coriander seeds

10 bay leaves

juice of another 10 lemons

Wash and slit the lemons into quarters without separating them at the base. In a sterilised jar, pack the lemons in tightly and add the salt, spices and lemon juice.

Seal the jar tightly and place in a very cool dark place for 3 months. To use, discard the flesh and pith of the lemons and rinse the rind.

oven-roasted tomatoes

250 ml (1 cup) olive oil

3 garlic cloves, peeled and finely sliced

12 sprigs of thyme

few stalks of basil

rock salt and pepper

12 roma tomatoes

Preheat oven to 80°C. Sprinkle the olive oil, garlic and the herbs on a roasting tray with the rock salt and pepper.

Cut the tomatoes lengthways and place them (cut face down) onto the tray.

Bake gently until nice and tender, about 5 hours. Peel the tomatoes and take out the seeds carefully. Set aside.

Keep in airtight container in fridge for up to 5 days.

pesto

2 cups of basil leaves, tightly packed

$1/4$ cup of pine nuts, toasted

extra virgin olive oil

1 cup of parmesan cheese, grated

Grind the basil in a mortar and pestle or a food processor. Add the pine nuts and then enough oil to make a smooth paste.

Add the parmesan cheese and a little more oil if necessary.

Store in an airtight container in fridge for up to 2 weeks.

olive tapenade

100 g ($3^1/_2$ oz) black olives

2 tbsp extra virgin olive oil

1 garlic clove, peeled and finely chopped

1 shallot, peeled and finely chopped

1 anchovy fillet, finely chopped

2 tsp parsley, finely chopped

freshly ground pepper

Pit the olives and cut them finely with a knife until you have a rough textured tapenade.

In 1 tablespoon of olive oil sweat the garlic, shallot and anchovy. Add the olives, the parsley and the remaining olive oil and cook slowly in order to release maximum flavour. Season with ground pepper only.

Tapenade will keep indefinitely if covered with oil and stored in a jar in the fridge.

red capsicum and basil oil

1 red capsicum

1/2 garlic clove, peeled and diced

6 basil leaves

2 tsp tomato paste

100 ml (3 1/2 fl oz) olive oil

salt and pepper

Dice the red capsicum with the garlic and the basil leaves and warm them with the olive oil over very low heat for about 15 minutes.

Remove from heat and let it infuse for a further 30 minutes. Strain through a cheesecloth and season.

Oil is best made just before use.

pickled cucumbers

6 baby cucumbers

500 ml (2 cups) water

75 ml (2 1/2 fl oz) rice vinegar

1 garlic clove, peeled and bruised

Peel and cut the cucumbers into julienned strips.

Bring the water, vinegar and garlic to the boil. Pour liquid over the cucumbers and leave to steep for 5 minutes.

Pickled cucmbers will keep indefinitely if stored in an airtight jar in the fridge.

duck confit

4 duck legs, knuckles chopped off

zest of 1 orange

zest of 1 lemon

1 bay leaf

1 pinch of crushed black pepper

100 g (3½ oz) sea salt

2 crushed juniper berries

1 litre (4 cups) rendered duck fat or
   olive oil

Wash duck and dry with paper towel then coat with mixture of orange zest, lemon zest, bay leaf, black pepper, sea salt and juniper berries.

Marinate duck in ovenproof dish (with lid on) in refrigerator for 24 hours.

Preheat oven to 140°C. Take duck legs from marinade, rinse under cold water, then dry with paper towel. Remove marinade from dish and wash clean. Place duck back into the clean ovenproof dish and add the duck fat (or olive oil if you have no access to duck fat).

Cook in oven for 2 hours or until meat is falling off the bones. Remove from oven and cool in the fat. Once cooled, remove from pan and discard skin and bones.

To keep, return meat into duck fat (ensuring that the meat is covered) then store in refrigerator with lid on for up to 1 month.

pork belly

500 g (1 lb) of pork belly

1 carrot

1 leek

1 onion

1 stick of celery

a bouquet garni

2 litres (8 cups) chicken stock
   (see recipe page 192)

Preheat oven to 160°C. Blanch the pork belly for 5 minutes in boiling water.

Roughly chop the vegetables and place in a fresh pot with the bouquet garni. Put the pork belly on top.

Half fill the pot with chicken stock and place a lid on the pot. Cook for 60 minutes in the oven, then turn the pork over and cook until a skewer meets no resistance when inserted.

Remove the pork. Allow to cool and refrigerate before slicing.

passionfruit custard

160 ml (5$^{1}/_{2}$ fl oz) fresh passionfruit
     pulp, strained and seeds reserved
100 ml (3$^{1}/_{2}$ fl oz) milk
1 vanilla bean
2 tsp sugar
2 tsp cornflour
3 egg yolks

Bring passionfruit juice to the boil and in another saucepan do the same with the milk, vanilla bean and sugar.

Combine the cornflour and yolks, thinning with a little fresh milk if necessary. Add to the boiling milk and cook until it is well combined, about 1 minute. Add the boiling passionfruit juice, cook until well combined, strain and chill. Add 1 teaspoon of passionfruit seed to the custard.

Store in the fridge for up to 3 days.

caramel sauce

150 g (5 oz) sugar
water (enough to make the sugar wet)
100 ml (3$^{1}/_{2}$ fl oz) glucose or golden
     syrup
250 ml (1 cup) cream
25 g (1 oz) butter

Cook the sugar, water and glucose to a dark caramel. Add the cream and bring back to the boil. Take off the heat and slowly whisk in the butter. Strain and cool.

Store in the fridge for up to 7 days in an airtight container.

coconut icecream

375 ml (1½ cups) milk

125 ml (½ cup) cream

100 g (3½ oz) desiccated coconut

125 ml (½ cup) coconut cream

115 g (4 oz) sugar

3 egg yolks

Boil milk, cream and coconut and let it sit so that the flavours can infuse for 1 hour. Strain and add the coconut cream.

Combine the sugar and egg yolks. Bring the coconut mixture back to the boil and add a touch of this liquid to the sugar and egg yolk mixture. Add the sugar and egg yolk mixture to the balance of the liquid. Cook slowly while stirring until mixture thickens and coats the back of a wooden spoon.

Strain and cool. Churn in an icecream machine and freeze.

pistachio crunch

50 g (1½ oz) brown sugar

100 ml (3½ fl oz) honey

50 ml (1½ fl oz) grapeseed oil

350 g (11 oz) rolled oats

175 g (6 oz) chopped pistachios

Preheat oven to 120°C.

Heat the sugar, honey and grapeseed oil over medium heat until sugar is dissolved. Pour mixture over the oats and pistachios. Mix well and spread over greased baking trays.

Bake for 40 minutes or until golden brown and crisp. Cool down and crunch gently in a plastic bag.

Store in an airtight container for up to 3 months.

GLOSSARY

bake blind

This prevents pastry from shrinking and pastry bases from becoming soggy. To bake blind, line a prepared tin with pastry, then cover with greaseproof paper and weigh down with dried beans or rice. Bake until pastry is just cooked, then remove paper and weights. Pour in prepared filling and return to oven to cook filling.

bakers flour

Also known as strong flour. It has a higher gluten content than plain or cake flour, and this produces light loaves with a soft crumb.

ballotine

Meat, chicken or fish that has been boned, stuffed, rolled and tied into a bundle.

bavette

A type of pasta that is basically a narrower form of linguine.

brandade

A flavourful purée made with fish, garlic, olive oil and milk.

brunoise

Very finely diced raw carrot, celery, leek or zucchini. It is traditionally used as a base for stews or soups or as a garnish for consommé.

cabicou

A type of goat's cheese.

carpaccio

Paper-thin shavings of raw meat or fish, traditionally drizzled with olive oil and lemon juice.

cassolette

A small individual cooking dish used to cook and present food.

crème fraîche

Matured thickened cream with a slightly tangy flavour.

egg wash

Gives bread or pastry a rich golden colour and a glossy glaze. It is also used to seal pastry before baking. Mix 1 egg yolk with 1 tablespoon water and whisk until well combined. Brush over pastry or bread just before baking.

fontina

An Italian cow's-milk cheese with a mild nutty flavour.

fromage blanc

An extremely soft fresh cheese that has the consistency of sour cream.

gorgonzola

A soft Italian blue cheese with a rich and creamy flavour.

harissa

This Tunisian spice blend is extremely hot and traditionally contains chillies, garlic, cumin and coriander.

julienne

Very long, thin matchstick slices of vegetables that require very little cooking.

maccheroni

More commonly known as macaroni, this pasta is shaped like little tubes.

mascarpone

An unripened rindless Italian cheese with the consistency of clotted cream.

panzotti

This pasta is triangular-shaped and stuffed, with pinked edges.

papillote

A French term that refers to food baked inside parchment paper.

rotolo

This pasta is shaped like a little wheel with spokes.

water bath

A French cooking technique where a container of food is placed in a larger shallow pan of water for cooking in the oven.

★ All recipes use large eggs with an average weight of 60 g (2 oz), unless otherwise stated.

CONVERSION CHART

One Australian metric tablespoon (tbsp) = 20 ml
One Australian metric teaspoon (tsp) = 5 ml
One cup = 250 ml (8 fl oz)

OVEN TEMPERATURES

	°C (Celsius)	°F (Fahrenheit)	Gas mark
Very slow	120	250	1
Slow	150	300	2
Moderately slow	160	325	3
Moderate	180	350	4
Moderately hot	200	400	5
Hot	220	450	6
Very hot	240	500	7

DRY AND LIQUID MEASURES

Metric (grams)	Imperial (ounces/pounds)	Metric (millilitres)	Imperial (fluid ounces)
30 g	1 oz	30 ml	1 fl oz
60 g	2 oz	60 ml	2 fl oz
90 g	3 oz	90 ml	3 fl oz
125 g	4 oz	125 ml	4 fl oz
150 g	5 oz	150 ml	5 fl oz
180 g	6 oz	180 ml	6 fl oz
200 g	7 oz	200 ml	7 fl oz
250 g	8 oz	250 ml	8 fl oz
280 g	9 oz	280 ml	9 fl oz
310 g	10 oz	310 ml	10 fl oz
340 g	11 oz	340 ml	11 fl oz
375 g	12 oz	375 ml	12 fl oz
500 g	16 oz / 1 lb	500 ml	16 fl oz
1 kg	32 oz / 2 lb	1 litre	32 fl oz

METRIC	IMPERIAL
Centimetres (cm)	**Inches (in)**
Millimetres (mm)	
2-3 mm	$1/8$ in
5-6 mm	$1/4$ in
1 cm	$1/2$ in
2 cm	$3/4$ in
2.5 cm	1 in
5 cm	2 in
6 cm	2 $1/2$ in
8 cm	3 in
10 cm	4 in
13 cm	5 in
15 cm	6 in
18 cm	7 in
20 cm	8 in
23 cm	9 in
25 cm	10 in
28 cm	11 in
30 cm	12 in

ACKNOWLEDGEMENTS

My parents introduced me to good food and taught me to respect great produce. My childhood was filled with the delicious tastes of wild blueberries, freshly caught fish, garden-fresh asparagus, rustic wild duck stew and hot-out-of-the-oven rhubarb pie. All these foods were based on fresh ingredients and it was an ideal upbringing to develop a love of good food.

The credit for my decision to become a chef goes to the chefs who trained me in Canada. Klaus, my first boss, marked me for life by his talent and work ethic and Daniel taught me passion for food, life and the power of flavours.

I thank Ted, my general manager at The Regent, Sydney, for entrusting me with too much responsibility, thereby making me a more resilient and focused chef. I thank Max for anchoring me in Australia and making me believe in myself at times of self-doubt. I thank my old kitchen team at The Regent for helping me achieve standards that were unheard of at the time.

I have to acknowledge my colleagues: the chefs who became friends, the suppliers who trusted me, the merchants who put up with my preaching and the growers who delivered produce even better than my dreams.

No people deserve my thanks more than my staff, past and present, at Bathers'. Each of them has contributed to our success and I'm proud to have them on my team. My chefs have worked so hard that they have redefined the word commitment; my service staff make us all look good; and my managers give me unflinching support.

Thanks need to go directly to the team who helped to produce this book: Ron, my ever supportive chef of many years, helped me define and cook the dishes; Cath, my editor, made recipe writing a breeze; Ingrid produced beautiful pages; Petrina captured the essence of Bathers' with her superb photos; Kristy, my assistant, managed us all; and Jane, my agent and team leader, kept us very focused.

Lastly, I have to thank Yvette, my beautiful wife, for always focusing me on the essence of my work, making sure the customers came first, and giving me joy and pleasures with her enthralling personality and unique 'joie de vivre'.

INDEX

Thanks go to
Accoutrement in Mosman, NSW, Village Living in Avalon Beach, NSW
and Malcolm Greenwood for the use of their beautiful tableware
and to
Kerrie Lester, James Willebrant, Crispin Akerman and Graham Monro
for the use of their artwork in the photographs

Published by ABC Books for the
AUSTRALIAN BROADCASTING CORPORATION
GPO Box 9994 Sydney NSW 2001

Copyright © Serge Dansereau 2004

First published October 2004

National Library of Australia
Cataloguing-in-publication entry
Dansereau, Serge, 1956-
The Bathers' Pavilion Café Cookbook
Includes index
ISBN 0 7333 1377 9
1. Cookery. I Australian Broadcasting Corporation.
II Title.
641.5

Produced by Jane Ogilvie
Designed by Ingrid Kwong
Photography by Petrina Tinslay
Colour reproduction by Colorwize, Adelaide
Printed and bound by Tien Wah Press, Singapore

2 4 5 3 1